Fathers & Sons

photographs, quotes and essays

Randy Snook

Visual Press

Special thanks go to the following individuals: Judy Bennett, Cathie Bradley, Jan Croom, Jatta Howell, Sue Knight, May Shen Krach, Craig Lomax, Shirley Queja, Lynne Rominger, Vance Slingsby, John Swain, Lynn Williams, my children Sara, Brian and Lauren, Ferrari Color Corporation for their outstanding digital negatives, Andrea Lepore and the Sacramento Kings' organization, Kimberly MacIntyre and Martha Robinson and the San Francisco 49ers' organization.

Library of Congress Cataloging in Publication Data:

Snook, Randy.
    Fathers & Sons: photographs, quotes and essays/ photographs by Randy Snook; design by Diane Sutherland. 1st ed.
    152p. 22.86 x 25.4 cm.
    ISBN: 0-9658272-2-4 (softcover)
    ISBN: 0-9658272-1-6 (hardcover)

    1. Fathers and sons—Photographs. I. Title. II. Title: Fathers and sons

HQ756.S66 1997   306.874'2'0222
                QBI97-40746

Printed in Korea by SUNG IN Printing

Visual Press
3385 Lanatt St., Suite B
Sacramento, CA 95819

Fathers & Sons

photographs, quotes and essays

by Randy Snook

Editor
Jenn Pfeiffer

Assistant Editors
Sue Lafferty Snook
Lisa Travers

Research Coordinator
Lisa Travers

Research Assistants
Bonny-Anne Fink
Laura Martin
H.B. Scott

Design by
Diane Sutherland

Introduction

The following pages are dedicated to some of the most important men in our world, fathers. Page after page will remind you of the value and importance of fathers in our society. I believe this reminder is necessary, because too often men do not take seriously the great responsibility they have in raising and nurturing their children. This book is filled with wonderful examples of commitment, appreciation and love, that will encourage and inspire you. Every relationship displayed is unique and intriguing, allowing us to see the diversity of relationships that exists around us.

My desire is that this book will go beyond being an interesting series of portraits and essays. By giving this book as a gift, it becomes a way in which fathers and sons can express their appreciation and love for each other. Expressing the value of a relationship is often a difficult thing for men to do, but this book will make it much easier. With this desire in mind, I have set aside the following page for a father or son giving this book as a gift, to write a few words to the recipient. I don't believe that the primary value is in the eloquence of what is said, but the value lies in the fact that *something* is said.

In addition, there is a page at the end of the book designed to make men aware of their need to have regular medical examinations for early detection of prostate cancer. Most men do not realize that the number one killer of fathers in our world today is prostate cancer. Please take the time to read this important information.

Finally, as you look through the pages that follow, I want to encourage you to take a moment to reflect on the value and importance that your father or son holds in your own life. More than anything, I hope that this book will help remind us of how much a father loves his son, and how a son needs his father.

Randy Snook

Personal Dedication

Preface

The blood of a father surges through his son's veins and the tide of two souls are etched as one, sure and strong, upon the shores of eternity.

Dad's reassuring smile for his boy about to take his first, uncertain steps; his soft, smiling eyes, which hold answers to so many questions his son has but never has to ask; Dad's soothing voice assuaging his son's fears in the dark; his strong arms offering safe harbor for his boy, adrift in the tumultuous seas of adolescence; a father's vision-a son's most reliable beacon, lighting a clearer tack across life's currents of confusion.

Memories of moments such as these are not enough. The Mathews Foundation for Prostate Cancer Research is committed to keeping Dad around so that the nurturing can continue.

Ben Schlossberg _____

George Seifert, *Professional Football Coach*
Jason Seifert, *Officer, U. S. Navy*

George Seifert: When I was young, I used to go fishing in the ocean with my dad a great deal. I introduced my son to the ocean at an early age. The ocean was something that my dad and I loved, and it has become a common thread for Jason and me. Even though we both have a love for the ocean, we have it in different ways. While I love to fish, he is an avid sailor, wind surfer, board sailor and surfer. So, while I am hoping for a nice calm day and flat water to go out in my powerboat, he's looking forward to a nice windy day to fill his sails.

We also share a fondness for the Trinity Alps. From the time Jason was a small boy we would go there every year. I remember him as a little guy, running around the creeks and hiking on the trails with me. About a year ago he learned how to fly and he took me up with him for the first time. He flew the plane into Trinity Center, and then over the Trinity Alps. It was mind-boggling that Jason was flying me in an airplane, when it was just a little while ago that he was this little guy hiking the trails and playing around in the water.

Jason has many individual passions of his own, and I feel good about that. I think it is a healthy thing, as opposed to him having to follow in my footsteps. I guess I didn't want my kids to be hung up on pro football. At least not to the point that it became their life. Because, I'm not going to be in this all my life, and I didn't want it to become theirs.

Jason Seifert: I think he's one of the best dads that a guy could have. My dad has always been really intense. He's intense about his career and about being a father. When he's being a coach, he's very focused and puts a great deal of effort into it. He's also like that when he's being a father, coaching me in a sense. Though he has been a great dad, he has also been somewhat intimidating to me, more so when I was younger than now. He tells me that I should do what I want and that I don't have to follow in his footsteps. Because of his great success, however, there has been this pressure that I have placed on myself to try and fill his shoes.

When I was a teenager, there was quite a bit of tension between us. As I get older, though, I see myself becoming more like him. I believe that we have a better understanding of each other now. We have many differences, but then, we are a lot alike. We're alike in the way that we think. I believe that we are both very strong minded. We both love the ocean, but again, we love it in different ways. My dad loves to fish, and I couldn't care less about fishing. I'd rather be sailing. Just total opposites. We do have this love for the water though, that binds us together. My dad and I can both sit on a bluff overlooking the ocean and just stay there, without saying a word, just enjoying the moment, for a very long time. I don't know many people like that, except my dad.

He's really proud of what I am doing. I'm really proud of him, too.

Philip Lee: One thing that I have always done with all of our boys is to be physical with them. We've always done a lot of "horsing around" (touching, hugging and tickling), and that continues with each of them. I want them to know my touch is caring, fun and humorous. I express my love for them in those physical ways.

Peter is the most athletic of the three, and he seems to love playing any sport he has an opportunity to. He's a "natural." He has golden eyes and thick blond hair. Nathan is the more creative of the three, always intrigued by details, noticing birds and animals in particular. He's sensitive and captivated by life. Nathan's eyes constantly invite interaction. Tim's a combination of those attributes. He's aggressive in athletics, yet emotionally sensitive and transparent. He has eyes that always reveal the emotions behind them.

One of the things I really appreciate about our boys is that they still kiss and hug me. They are all affectionate, without any sense of awkwardness or being self-conscious. It nurtures and strengthens me, and gives me profound satisfaction and appreciation for each of them.

As a Christian, I believe very strongly that faith should be expressed in action. One way I do that is in my relationship with our three boys. I attempt to be honest with my failures as a person and in my role as a father, especially when I blow it with them by expressing my anger by shouting at them and intimidating them. When I'm wrong, I try hard to recognize it and admit it to them, because I believe that honesty and forgiveness foster open and loving relationships for a lifetime. Finally, at the end of each day, with a sense of awe and humility and thanksgiving, I commit my children and my whole family to the Lord in prayer.

Peter Lee: My Dad's a pastor. When somebody sings a solo or the choir sings, he always closes his eyes. I like to be like him, so I do that, too.

Nathan Lee: My dad kisses us good night, and he hugs us a lot.

Tim Lee: Some nights my dad goes in my brother's room and hides from us. He turns the light off in the hallway, so when one of my brothers goes in the room he goes, "Boo!" It's fun when he does that.

BA Robertson, *Songwriter*
Rory Robertson

The Living Years

Every generation
Blames the one before
And all of their frustrations
Come beating on your door.

I know that I'm a prisoner
To all my father held so dear
I know that I'm a hostage
To all his hopes and fears
I just wish I could have told him
In the living years.

Crumpled bits of paper
Filled with imperfect thought
Stilted conversations
I'm afraid that's all we've got.

You say you just don't see it
He says it's perfect sense
You just can't get agreement
In this present tense
We all talk a different language
Talking in defense.

Say it loud, say it clear
You can listen as well as you hear
It's too late when we die
To admit we don't see eye to eye.

So we open up a quarrel
Between the present and the past
We only sacrifice the future
It's the bitterness that lasts.

So don't yield to the fortunes
You sometimes see as fate
It may have a new perspective
On a different day
And if you don't give up,
and don't give in
You may just be OK.

Say it loud, say it clear
You can listen as well as you hear
It's too late when we die
To admit we don't see eye to eye.

I wasn't there that morning
When my father passed away
I didn't get to tell him
All the things I had to say.
I think I caught his spirit
Later that same year
I'm sure I heard his echo
In my baby's new born tears
I just wish I could have told him
In the living years.

6

Kent Nuzum: When my father died, I was ten years old. I remember that I was playing with my yo-yo when I found out. I kept trying to get it to stay straight on the planks of my front porch. I kept thinking that if I got the yo-yo straight, that my dad wouldn't be dead anymore. It never would go straight for me...

....My father was affectionate. I remember that sometimes he would come in from the fields and have his meal. He would then take a nap and I would fall asleep on his chest. I remember sleeping like that until I was seven or eight years old.

Rabbi Cohen: The Jewish faith affects your perspective on fatherhood. In the Bible, it says that the obligation of education belongs to the father. You have to teach them everything that you have learned. It is not enough to pay tuition to a school and allow your obligation to end there. The foundation of what kids get is in the home. Also, because of the Hasidic teaching of selfless dedication to God, there should also be a selfless dedication to your children. My children are blessings from God. Both of them only bring me happiness and joy. My children have the most beautiful smiles and Peretz has such a wonderful glow in his eyes.

" The foundation of what kids get is in the home. Also, because of the Hasidic teaching of selfless dedication to God, there should also be a selfless dedication to your children."

יום ראשון, כ"ו אדר. בריקודים היומיים של חודש זה נוסף הערב חידוש מעניין: א' התמימים (הת' יוסף יצחק שי' סילבר... השמיע בפעם הראשונה את השיר ל'קאפיטל' של הרבי. השיר מ... הפסוקים הראשונים של מזמ... בתהילים, ובסיומו, כמובן, הכרז... "יחי". השיר השמח התק... הקהל שהצטרף לניגון.

יום שני, ז"ך א... והאמונה האיתנ... ...ודות החיים הנצחיים של הרבי – בא", שררה ...ינו לא מת" ובעוד שלמצרים "נדמה שהתקיים הערב הרג... ...ומת" הרי בני יעקב ידעו ש"לא מת" המר והתביעה והנחיש... ...ינו לדעת כבני יעקב.

...ומים עבר הקהל לריקוד ...טה שירה וזמרה" ולאחר התוועדות חסידית.

...ניסן. לאחר השיעור ...ות כ"ק אד"ש מה"מ ...ית לתלמידי הקבוצה ...' ליברוב, שליח כ"... ...טבוש, שעורר את ...רבות לא לשקוט ולא ...בי בעיני-בשר.

...אחר התפילה והכרזת ...נו מורנו ורבינו מלך ...הודיע הגבאי על ...שתיערך אי"ה ...הבהיר י"א ניסן.

שעובר ו"עדיין לא בא"! הת' חיים שי' ברנד חזר על שיחת כ"ק אד"ש מה"מ מש"פ ויקהל ה'תשנ"ב והר' יצחק גנזבורג דיבר על הצורך ...פיץ את המעיינות באמצעות קלטות ווידאו ...יל לפעמים יותר מדיבור בלבד.

...במשל מעניין ובדברים היוצאים מן הלב ...יאר הת' אורי שי' למברג את ההרגשה ...חת כי הרבי הוא חיינו ולכן אין אנו ...בשום אופן לחשוב על המחר ללא הרבי,

...ח"ו, ולסיום דיבר הת' אסף שי'

מבעוד מועד הוזמ... להשתתף בכינוס, וא... חסידות כאשר התמי... במקומותיהם נטל הת' ...את שבט ההנחיה והזמ... שי' סילברמן לפתוח ב... קישר את המובא בשי... הזריזות הדרושה מיהודי ל... לשיחה האחרונה לע"ע של... על הצורך בהוספה באה... באופן של "אדם כי יקריב... עצמית. הרב שלמה שי' שפ... עורר אודות הצורך והנחת... גאולה ומשיח ולערוך ת...

...נו... ...יחי ה... ...המשיה ...התוועד...

והאמונה האיתנה שתיכף ומיד ממש "הנה זה בא", שררה ב'כינוס התמימים' המיוחד

...הודעה הגבאי על ...תיערך אי"ה ...בהיר י"א ניסן. ...פרומר אודות החיים הנצחיים של הרבי – "יעקב אבינו לא מת" ובעוד שלמצרים "נדמה

Earl Self, *Contractor*
Michael Self, *Programmer Analyst*

Earl Self: I am the father of seven children, four of which are boys. It is an awesome responsibility to raise a family of that size, with its many burdens and rewards. I have the usual memories of childhood diseases, nose-bleeds and first dates. But, my fondest memories are of working side by side with three of my sons in a business we owned. You must be ready for three steps forward and one step backwards when you embark on such a venture.

We had the privilege of seeing many projects through, from concept to completion. But, the best times we had together were at lunch. It was a time to set aside the aggravations of the job and just be friends. We shared jokes and laughter, our goals for the future and our dreams.

The best years of my life were spent working with my sons. It wasn't that every day went well. But, we never allowed a problem to carry over to the next day. My greatest challenge was knowing when to be the Father, and when to defer judgment to the boys who were becoming men right before my eyes.

My son, Michael, and I have had the longest and closest relationship. Although we have very different natures, we have learned the give and take that is necessary to maintain a good relationship. The give and take didn't come easy for either one of us. The struggle was sometimes very intense and unpleasant, with power changing hands regularly. However, we were always able to resolve our differences because of the love and respect we have for each other.

Michael is now in college and has a great future ahead of him, which does not include working with his dad. My other sons have likewise gone on to bigger and better things. I feel fortunate, though, because I have had the joy of working shoulder to shoulder with my sons, and we have been partners and friends. How could you ask for more?

Michael Self: My father has a great proclivity for story-telling. He loves to tell stories about his youth and the experiences he had. Working with him, I have heard him tell these stories many times. Something important passes between us each time a story is told. I think he not only enjoys the telling, but the fact that I care enough to listen, even though we both know I have heard the tale before, and enjoy hearing them again.

It is difficult to describe the respect I have for my father and his abilities. Indeed, this has often been the source of much conflict between us. It's the old story of the son trying to prove himself to the father. Although we long ago passed through the major focus of this conflict, working together has often forced this issue to resurface. I think I have learned more about myself from having to deal with this than I have from anything else.

Henry Robinett: I made a promise when my first child was born, and reconfirmed it the when the second arrived. For their part the bargain is simple. They only have to share as much of their life with me as they choose. For my part, I promise to be there for Charles and Landon for the rest of my life. I will provide guidance and nourishment, and maintain a high level of communication and a profound interest in their lives. Though I will provide them with guidance, I will also give them the space to make their own decisions. I wrote a song I call "The Gift" on my CD *When Fortresses Fall* that was inspired by this promise.

I've learned such an incredible amount from my children. Patience and anger. Love and caring. I'm surprised that I'm not as selfish as I used to be. I'll find myself all alone, passing a toy store, and then going back just to see what new toys I can bring home to my boys.

Mornings are about the only time I can steal for myself at home. I arise about five-thirty a.m. to practice; an unheard of hour for most musicians. Charles or Landon, but usually Charles, will wake up around seven a.m. and crawl up into my lap, forcing me to put my guitar down. This is one of my most enjoyable times. We just hug, talk and sit together.

Recently, Charles did something he has rarely done; he failed to make it to the bathroom in time. Not just once, but two nights in a row. His mother was away on business for almost two weeks. I attribute these mishaps to her absence. The second night he didn't make it to the bathroom, he just got out of bed and stood there urinating. Actually, he was peeing all over his mother's cellular telephone that was on the floor getting recharged.

"Charles," I yelled, "What are you doing? Charles!" In his almost-sleep state, he was so shocked that I was raising my voice with him, that he just started crying, "Daddy I love you!" This broke my heart.

Landon has, from the beginning, staked ownership in Daddy. He wants to play the guitar. He always points out that his daddy plays the guitar. Landon is a very sweet boy, as is Charlie. Landon is full of such unrelenting personality, and he makes me laugh. I just have to kiss them both all the time. They bring me such joy.

If you were to ask them about me, they might say that their daddy is very silly. If one of them gets hurt, I become "Dr. Daddy." I pick them up and lay them on their beds. I feel for their injury, while trying to maintain a semi-serious doctor-like manner. Gently, I tickle them while saying, "Umm. Let's see if Dr. Daddy can fix this." They laugh their heads off.

Becoming a father has helped me to realize how important a role fathers play in their children's lives. Too often we men have absconded from what is arguably our primary responsibility, fatherhood. A lot of talk goes on about the derailment of the contemporary family, and at its root, the lack of fathers in the home. No doubt about it, we men have had our major league shortcomings. I believe this is the age of women. They have grown, and have forced our hand. They have caused us to confront ourselves. But even more so, it's our children who force our hand. They are the gentle souls who put their faith, trust and undying love in us, their fathers. It is up to us to not let them down.

Bill Lomax: Craig was sent to us after I had thought our family was complete. I'm glad God knew better and blessed me with this wonderful son. He has given us nothing but pride and joy.

I've encouraged him to be satisfied only when his good was better and his better best. My observation now is he works too hard at this endeavor, seeking perfection in his work and relationships with both God and family.

So many memories are special it's difficult to choose. He achieved success in swimming, cross country, scouts, and 4H, especially his goats. He was dedicated and faithful to these and other activities. School was not easy for him, but he completed both high school and college with high marks.

A story he recalls often occurred on one of our many camping trips. I was backing into a campsite in my new camper and failed to hear his little voice shouting, "Stop Dad! Stop! There's a tree!" As I heard the crunch of metal and wood I also heard him mutter, "No one ever listens to me!" Well, we do now.

Craig Lomax:

My father kept the walls standing
   and the cars running
He kept his word
   and he kept his wife

He kept my stomach full
   and my body warm
He kept discipline at hand
   and God in his heart

Now he is in Autumn
   and like a leaf he is changing
As the days grow shorter
He has become less a mystery
   and much more a friend

Though his body is failing
   his heart has grown wings
The strength of his love
   is growing stronger by the day

I've decided I am not going to wait
   any longer
I want a heart like his today

Olden Polynice: My son is ten months old and he's the happiest baby. It is amazing that we have him. There were complications after his birth because he was two months premature. Being there during his birth gave me a whole different perspective. It was a wonderful experience that I believe every man should have.

When I'm on the road, I really miss seeing him on a daily basis, but when I am home he looks at me and I feel everything else just disappears. I know

there is somebody right there who needs me. He is my base. Everything else, win, lose or draw, really doesn't matter.

I don't think I'm that much different than my father or even my grandfather. My father and grandfather taught me by their actions that family always comes first. My father made great sacrifices for his family. He had to struggle and work hard to get us out of Haiti. My father went alone to the United States and worked for two years to save enough money to send for my mother. The two of them had to work for another two years before they could send for my siblings and me. It was very hard being apart from my father for that long.

Like any father, I have dreams for my son. I will, of course, support anything he does, but I tend to picture him using his mind, not his body to succeed in life. I know my job is not to choose his future for him, but only to lay a foundation, give him choices and make sure he knows right from wrong.

Nikolas goes to every home game. I'm not sure how much he sees or understands, but I know he's there. When I look up and see him and acknowledge him, right before I go out, that helps me more than anything else.

General H. Norman Schwarzkopf, *U. S. Army, Retired*
Christian N. Schwarzkopf, *College Student*

General H. Norman Schwarzkopf: After I retired, Christian and I became best friends, buddies really. Then, a couple of years ago he got some wheels and discovered girls. So, we didn't spend quite as much time together, but we still are very close. We try to go fishing in Alaska together for two weeks every year and our family gets together to ski in the winter. One of my fondest memories of Christian was when we went fishing in Alaska together. Christian was around eleven years old at the time. We were on a boat, with a guide, fishing for Red Salmon. They usually weigh around fifteen pounds and put up a nice fight. Well, Christian hooked a forty-eight pound King Salmon. As he was bringing it in, I would have to continually turn the boat, and each time I went behind him, I would give the pole a little tug. When he landed the fish, the guide and I were slapping him on the back congratulating him. But, he said it didn't count because I had helped him. So, he threw his line back in the water and he hooked a fifty-two pound King Salmon and he brought it in all by himself. His fish were bigger than anything I caught.

Christian Schwarzkopf: When I did something wrong my father let me know it, but he was not overly strict or too harsh. People often have asked me if my father was really tough, but he wasn't. Recently, I had an experience where I observed people acting on their prejudice. I knew that they were acting in that manner because of the way they were raised. I later told my parents how grateful to them I was for the way in which they raised me, with a good core of values and morals, which included zero tolerance for prejudice.

Conrad Murdock, *Farmer*
Burton Murdock

Conrad Murdock: I don't understand why my son had to die before me...

Frank LaPena: As a young child, I was separated from mother after my father was killed. I was then put into the Federal Indian Boarding School system in Nevada and later in Oregon. Then I was placed into a foster home and had to wait until after I graduated from high school to locate some of my relatives, which I did. I married a woman with five children and we had one girl and one boy together.

Both of my children have turned out very well, and I appreciate both of them. Because I am involved in California tribal activities and traditions, it makes me happy to say they are, as well.

My son Craig (Vince) is a very fine dancer and a good singer. In fact, he remembers songs better than I do. I enjoy singing with him, very much. Being able to share traditions with others is important, but to share them with family is truly special!

Vince LaPena: My dad has been instrumental in getting me involved in the culture of my people, the Wintu and also the Maidu. He started me off when I was a little kid by taking me to different elder's houses and the different ceremonies that my people have been having for generations.

When I was a kid, I didn't really see my dad's humorous side too much. I always thought he was so serious when I was growing up. Of course, he had six other kids to take care of, and I was a pretty independent kid, so I wasn't always around to see when he was really happy. But, as I've grown older, I've learned that this guy isn't as serious as I thought he was. We have had more time to just sit down and talk and even have a good laugh every once in a while.

My dad went through a lot of rough times when he was growing up. Because of that, when we got whiny about how tough things were, he would definitely set us straight! He would use his personal experiences and those of other people in other parts of the world, or even people just down the street, to make us realize that we didn't have anything to be whining about. That helped me realize the importance of what I have, instead of what I don't have. My dad instilled in me an appreciation for life and what it has to give you, not for the material possessions, but for the people in your life.

My dad was the one who got me into dancing in the beginning. His art has always been his main thing and the dancing and ceremonies have always been my main thing. That's one thing my dad has given me, an appreciation for art in all its forms. I feel as if I've been given the responsibility to carry on the dancing, so he can focus on his art. When we do our ceremonies, most of the time either my Dad is singing or I'm singing. But, every once in a while, we get to sing together, and that's always special.

Brian Sullivan: I don't know whether it's like this for everybody who adopts, but to me Dustin is my kid. I love him and I'm excited when he does great things. I also get upset when he doesn't behave. We're just like a regular family. It's only been three and a half years since Dustin came to live with us, but it seems much longer. I can't remember what life was like before Dustin came to live with us, and I don't want to.

Being a father has been a big adjustment for me. I used to be wild. I was used to doing things on my own when I wanted to. Now I have a family, and that comes first. I want Dustin to learn how to do the right thing. If he learns nothing else from me, I want him to believe in God and know right from wrong. Some people think I'm a little strict with Dustin, but I want him to have values.

I'm a roofer and I've watched other guys that I work with get into the business because their dads made them roof. I'm not going to do that with Dustin. I want him to stay in school and get a good education.

I have a Harley, but it stays in the garage most of the time. Before I was married, I used to ride every day. One time, when I was taking my Harley for a ride, my wife heard Dustin say, "Did you see my dad? He's so cool!" That really did make me feel like I was pretty cool. You see, when I was a kid, my dad would ride his motorcycle home from work and I'd wait for him on the porch. He'd do a wheely coming up to the house and I thought he was the coolest guy in the whole world. I hope Dustin will always look at me the same way I used to look at my dad.

" I love him and I'm excited when he does great things."

Randy Snook, *Commercial Photographer*
Brian Snook

Randy Snook:

Looking at your photograph
I see myself in your eyes
And in your heart

I put my arms around you
To remind you of how close we are
Not wanting to be apart for long

You have begun to push me away
Just a little
To a safe distance
Where you can grow

Still, you are close enough
That I can catch you if you fall
And push you when you stall

As days turn into years
Always remember that I am here
To wipe away the tears
And celebrate your triumphs

Always providing a safe haven
And a place of rest
Away from the storms of life

Then turning you around once more
And sending you on to be
Someone greater
Then I will ever be

Brian Snook: My dad is special because he spends a lot of time with me. My dad always wants to make me happy, so he does the things I like to do. He coaches my soccer team and plays basketball with me every night. My dad also spends time with me by tucking me in and reading stories to me every night. He's also taken me on trips and taught me how to fish. I love spending time with my dad and I can tell he loves spending time with me. I know that my dad loves me because he is very affectionate towards me and cares about everything I am doing.

John Showers: When my sons were very young, not quite in grade school, my marriage was not going very well. After three attempts to make it work, my marriage ended in divorce. There was a lot of fighting going on between my wife and me, and to make a long story short, she and her new boyfriend left the state with my children and didn't tell me where they were going. They kept this information from their friends and neighbors as well. I tried to find them, but I was unsuccessful.

After many years had passed, two of my sons, Norman and Ron, contacted me. Unless you are a father who has lost his children, I don't believe there is any way you could understand my emotions. There was still one son, Roscoe, that I wanted to make contact with. But, at that time in his life, he wanted nothing to do with me. This really hurt. All I wanted to do was tell him how much I loved him and his brothers and how sorry I was for the way things turned out, and that I did try to find them. Even though I was in contact with Ron and Norman, we were still not close and I was desperately trying to establish a good relationship with them.

Finally, with encouragement from Norman and Ron, and the wife of my youngest son, Roscoe, I was able to fly to Georgia to my son Norman's home for Christmas and meet Roscoe. My heart was pounding when I arrived and everyone was pretty tense. I remember putting my arms around my son and he did the same, but I could also feel the hurt and bitterness he felt towards me. For awhile it was just chit-chat between Norman, Roscoe, and me. Then it was time for some serious talk. Roscoe looked me right in the eye and asked me, "Why did you let me get adopted?" I was at a loss for words. I tried to explain to him that I had never given anyone permission to adopt him, and that he could not have been adopted. At that point we were finally able to sit down and have a good father and son discussion. There were so many things that I wanted to say and do in so little time. We did what would probably seem silly to some people, but was important to me. I sat them down on my lap and hugged them. I took them fishing and baited their hooks. Later that evening I told them to quiet down and go to sleep (remember these are grown men with wives and children). We all laughed and things quieted down. The second greatest thing that has happened is that all three of my sons have accepted my wife as their "Mom." This was never discussed, it just fell in place naturally. It was the boy's decision to call her "Mom".

Now we are a family and even though we are spread out all over the United States, we keep in constant contact. My wife and I get things in the mail that we save and cherish. Like birthday cards, anniversary cards, and letters from all ten of our grandchildren. When I look back, I feel that I am probably the luckiest man in the world. I have a wonderful wife of twenty years, three fantastic sons, great daughters-in-laws, and ten beautiful, healthy grandchildren. Finally, my son Roscoe has had his name changed to "Showers". What more could a man want?

I would like to conclude with some advice for parents. Never put your children in the position where they have to choose between Mom and Dad. Never give up your name, for it will come back and haunt you when you get older, and never give up hope for whatever reason if you think you have lost them. If you follow these rules, things will turn out okay. I can vouch for that.

" Children today are tyrants. They contradict their parents, gobble their food, and tyrannize their teachers."

Socrates

Fess Parker: To me, one of life's greatest gifts has been watching my son grow to manhood. I'm privileged to know him as a man and as a partner in our family business. To this day, I tell him that I love him. For me, there is still an element of surprise that he has a beautiful wife and five delightful daughters and two sons. He's talented, works hard and enjoys success. Most would agree that it is as it should be in life. However, historically it has been extremely difficult for children of celebrity parents. The culture and drugs have claimed many victims. I'm proud that he found his way.

As a father, I have tried to give the support my father gave to me. What a joy it is to see that my son is a good father.

Eli Parker: As I sit and look at my newborn son, I hope that someday he will see in me all of the positive things that I see in my father. I remember as a small boy being asked, "What is it like to have 'Davy Crockett' for a father?" or, "What is it like to have a celebrity father?" To me, he was just a great dad. There were so many fun times that we shared together and I will always remember and be thankful for the fact that my dad always had time for me. As I grew older and struggled for some independence, he was supportive of my actions and was always there when I needed him (even though I'm sure he thought I was crazy at times). Now that I'm grown and have children of my own, I hope I can be the teacher and role model that he still is for me.

A few years ago my dad and I, along with the rest of our family, started a small business. It has been the best experience of my life. I love working with him and look forward to someday having my children work with me. He has always been a great dad and now he is a great friend and business partner as well.

Wesley Rose, *Account Executive*
Paul Rose, *Student*

Wesley Rose: I never had the opportunity to live with my father, so I always promised myself that if I ever had a son, I would try to spend valuable time with him and help him avoid the mistakes I made as I was growing up. Not having a father, I missed out on advice about the character of a man, relationships with girls, how to run a household and so many other things. It would have been great just to able to have a father to talk to. There are things that are easier for a father to talk to his son about, in the same way that only a mother can really talk to her daughter about certain subjects. I care about Paul's life, and give him advice that I hope will help him to be happy and successful. I'm sure my father would have done the same, if he would have had the chance. I'm so glad I have been able to give to Paul what I never had.

Paul Rose: My dad has always been supportive of the things I do. From managing my baseball team, to encouraging me in my writing. A career in journalism is what I have chosen for my life. My dad always gives me encouragement when I show him my writing. When I was in elementary school, around second grade, I remember telling all the kids that my dad was a giant (he's six feet tall). We lived right across the street from the school. Everyone would look over and he would wave. The kids would say, "Wow, he is big." I also remember calling him my best friend. There is definitely some sadness as I prepare to leave my father and go off to college. But, it's something I have to do. He will always remain, though, a "giant" in my eyes.

" There are things that are easier for a father to talk to his son about, in the same way that only a mother can really talk to her daughter about certain subjects."

David Wittenborn: There is no adequate way to express the emotion I felt when I held my son, my first born, in the delivery room. Only thirty minutes earlier, I was signing papers to clear the way for my wife to have an emergency C-section. But after the papers were signed, the birth process, which hadn't progressed for hours, suddenly began again. So, we were whisked into the delivery room and everything progressed normally to my great relief. Holding my son was incredible. I tried to notice every detail of his tiny face. But it was his eyes that held my attention. There were bright overhead lights in the delivery room which caused many reflections on the shiny stainless steel rails and surfaces typical of hospital equipment. As I gently rocked him, his eyes would fix on the bright surface and grow wide with wonder. He would follow the reflection with his eyes as I moved with him. He was taking it all in. His expression reflected curiosity. He seemed to be thinking, "What is all this? Such brightness! What is going on here?" All the time, he rested contently in my arms and, after a few minutes, in the arms of his mother. But for the longest time, he just stared at everything around him. I thought to myself, "This baby is in awe. He is curious. How amazing that a newborn baby would have wonder and curiosity."

Daniel has always been curious. He questions everything and doesn't take anything for granted. It's been that way since Day One. I've never been able to keep up with all his questions. Most young children go through a phase at about age three of asking "Why?" Daniel entered that phase early, and hasn't outgrown it after thirteen years.

One area Dan is really good at is art. Since both his mother and I work with younger children, there are times when we need to prepare art work for projects or classroom decorations. It doesn't take me long to feel that I'm in over my head with drawing. So, we call on Dan. "Can you draw something for me?" A year ago for Father's Day, he sketched my portrait. It's one of my favorites. He depicted me with my paddle and life jacket which I use for whitewater rafting. He knew this was one of my favorite hobbies, and it is one he is learning also.

Dan and I both enjoy outdoor adventures. We belong to a Boy Scout troop which has provided many of those adventures. One summer, we went to Idaho and learned how to kayak. Dan also learned how to canoe in rivers. I remember watching with some trepidation as he traversed a swift-flowing river by himself in a canoe. On his return traverse, he had a difficult time maneuvering from the current into the eddy. I wondered if he would roll the canoe, but he seemed to know instinctively how to counter the current reversals, but he was still having trouble getting out of the downstream current. After getting pushed back into the current a few times, he kept the canoe headed correctly and persisted until he succeeded. It gave me a feeling of pride and reassurance that he didn't give up.

41

Dan Wittenborn: There are many things my dad and I enjoy doing together, especially outdoor activities. I think it is because we not only like adventurous things, but we like to marvel at God's creation as well. In the summer when my dad isn't teaching, he guides whitewater rafting trips. Sometimes I get to go with him and he is now teaching me how to guide.

We also enjoy rock climbing and animals. Whenever I have trouble with my iguana or snake, he is always there to help me. I remember when my snake escaped in the house one night and I quietly called my dad into my room, to see if he could help me with the situation. Well, mom got suspicious and came into my room to see what was going on. When she asked, my dad and I just looked at each other and when we didn't answer, she knew there was trouble. "The snake escaped, didn't it ?", she asked. After we answered yes, she jumped on top of a chair and in all seriousness threatened to stay in a hotel until the snake was found. She said that she was going to use the money in *my* bank account to pay the hotel bill. My poor dad was stuck between comforting my mom and finding my pet. Luckily I found my snake, Ginger, a few minutes later behind the T.V. That just shows you the stuff my dad has to deal with.

_____

Miniature,
by Richard Armour

My day-old son is plenty scrawny,

His mouth is wide with screams, or yawny;

His ears seem larger than he's needing,

His nose is flat, his chin's receding,

His skin is very, very red,

He has no hair upon his head,

And yet I'm proud as proud can be,

To hear you say he looks like me.

43

Mel Losoya: My father was an inspiration to me. He lived hard and worked hard. He was proud of his heritage, and he was proud of his family. He taught me the importance of what we do and what we say. His lessons came in various ways, often through the songs he sang and the stories he told. He was a positive influence on my life, and was always there to help me. My desire is to be the same type of influence in my sons' lives, that my father was in mine.

Melton Losoya: My dad has made his family very proud. He was recently elected to serve on the city council, and will become the first Latino Mayor of Woodland. Though my father is a very busy man with his city service and his job, he always has time for his family. As I was growing up I knew I could always count on him, and I still can. Whether I was working on my pitching, throwing a football around or doing my homework, my dad was always there to help me. I thank God for blessing me with a man I am very proud to call my dad.

Jason Losoya: My father is a man with a great heart and a lot of knowledge. He likes to joke and have fun, which is better than being serious all of the time. He helps and cares for his family, and works hard at his job. In fact, he does more for us than he does for himself. He has also helped others by having them stay in our home. I am proud of him for doing that. I know a lot of people are in awe of and look up to movie stars, football players and other famous people, but that is the way I feel about my dad.

Marcos Losoya: Even though my dad is very busy, he always has time for me. Even though he may come home tired from work, he will still help me work on my pitching, or come to my game. Every night he makes sure my bed is ready, and every morning he feeds me breakfast and takes me to school.

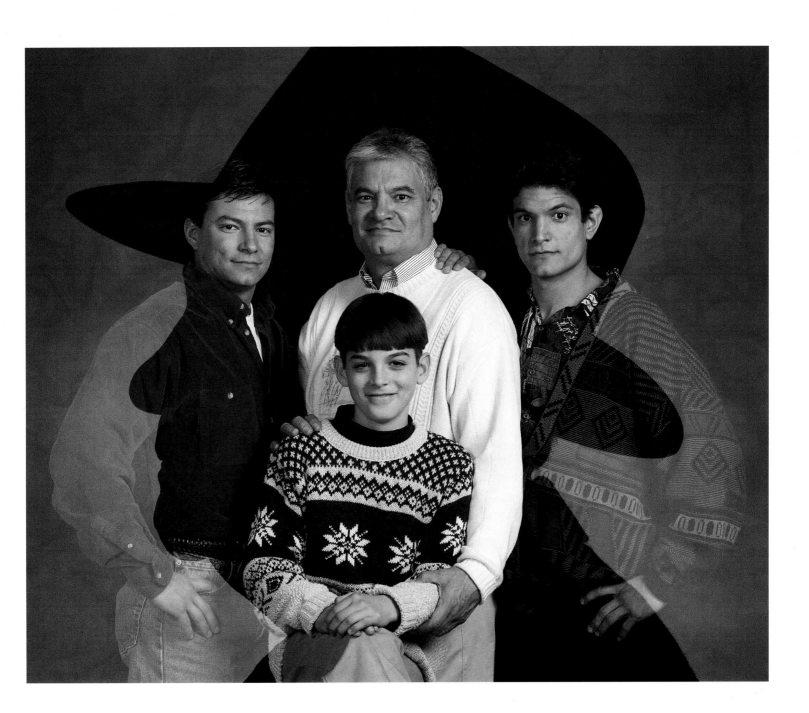

Derwin Terry: Being a dad is one of the most rewarding responsibilities I have had. I really enjoy being with them. I love Tony's honesty, politeness and caring. He is really a very deep person. Every day when I come home from work, he is there to greet me at the door. The first thing he says is, "Daddy I love you." Three or four times during the day he will say, "Guess what Daddy? I love you!" The thing I like the most about my youngest son, Troy, is his curiosity. I also love his laugh and the way he likes to dance all the time. I think Troy will be a private investigator. He's always looking for stuff, and finding it.

Tony Terry: I want to be a policeman and go in the street when I grow up. My dad likes taking pictures of me and he reads me stories.

" I want to be a policeman and go in the street when I grow up."

46

Sändor Tiche: "When you get angry like that, it makes my heart sad," my older son said to me when I asked his forgiveness for losing my temper. I learned that day how deep the feelings of understanding and love are that flow between us. I looked so forward to having a son to share with, that I used to have him help me mow the yard from the baby carrier on my back, before he could even walk. My younger son touched my heart the day he sang "The Lord's Prayer" at two years of age. This is the same son who also greets me when I come home by pointing his little finger at me and demanding emphatically, "Daddy, you wessel wit me."

I wish to teach my sons all I know and for us to learn and experience new ideas and activities together. My goal is to be their father and their friend in such a pleasant and loving way that the idea of a Heavenly Father is an appealing one and easy to embrace. I am excited by the future we have together and enjoy every day with my sons.

Dirk Tiche: My favorite thing about my dad is that he wrestles with me. I love him bigger than the whole outer space!

Nicholas Tiche: I love my dad bigger than a Tyrannosaurus Rex!

Dan Eichhorn, *Loan Officer*
Augustus Leueque-Eichhorn

Dan Eichhorn: Having a son has been one of the best things that has ever happened to me. I never thought I could feel such an intense and unconditional love for someone as I do for Gus. It was so incredible seeing him born, touching him, cutting his umbilical cord and staying with him the whole time he was in the nursery. That first night, Julie, Gus and I slept together at the hospital and three years later we're still sharing our bed with him. He likes to sleep in the middle but he is always kicking off the covers, so I insist he sleeps on the other end until around six when he gets in the middle and we snuggle up together.

I have a great job as a loan officer so my schedule is very flexible. It allows me to spend a lot of time with Gus. I am with him every other Friday and a half a day on Mondays. Sometimes he comes with me on my sales calls. A couple of months ago we took the light rail train down to the state capitol. It was the first time we both had been there and we had a great time. We checked out all of the historical rooms and walked up the grand staircase and went into the assembly chambers. The joke of the day was "Where's Pete?" and "Hey Pete, put some more money in the schools." Last month, we sent a letter to Pete (Governor Wilson) about the state of our coastline waters and what we can do to clean them up. We're still waiting for his reply.

Gus has an incredible fascination with trains. He plays with his wooden train set for hours. He likes to "break track," which is taking apart the old track and setting up a new one. He'll have his track going all over our living room-under the chairs, around the couch and under the coffee table. We also read train books, watch train movies and ride real trains. He has quite an imagination and will hook up just about anything to make a train out of it. The other morning he lined up his raisins in his cereal to make a train. We have a saying in our home, "trains, trains, trains on our brains."

I look forward to the many years ahead I'll share with Gus, especially times when I am teaching him to ride a bike, read, ski, fish, hike, backpack, play baseball and restoring an old truck for him to learn to drive. I tell him I love him at least three or four times a day and I hope I will be able to say "I love you" to him when he is a grown man. I would do just about anything for him. He says to me a lot, and I to him, "You're my best friend." He also says it to his mom, his cousin Sal, his Poppy (grandpa) and a few other special people. Someday, I hope he says it just to me.

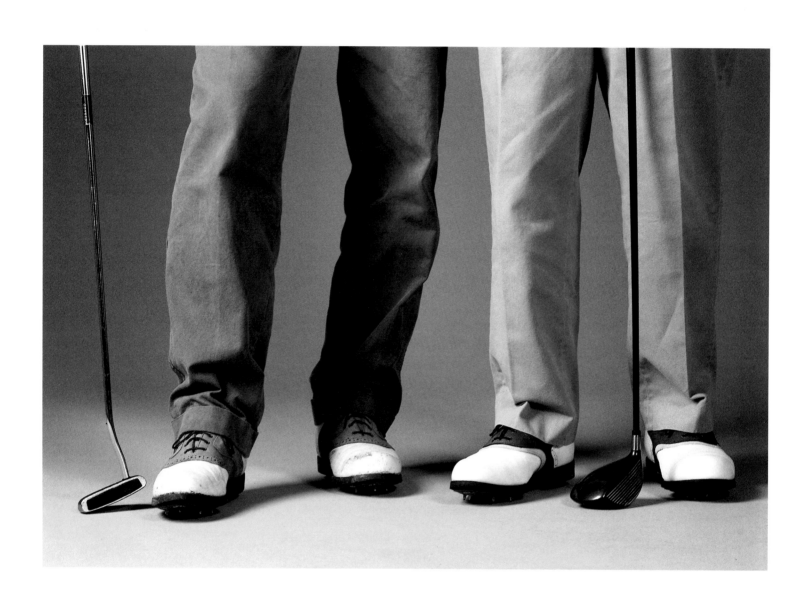

Bert Lee: I feel fortunate that I have such a good relationship with my three sons and my daughter. Having been separated from my parents by the Sino-Japanese War, I spent my formative years at my grandmother's home (which consisted mainly of women). A father's role was foreign to me, which was probably a poor excuse for spending very little time with my children while I became caught up in the post World War II era of pursuing the American Dream of financial success. All too soon, my older children were in high school or leaving for college. I was then faced with a deadline to play, what at that time I perceived, a fatherly role. Ronald being the youngest, was practically the only one left. He became the recipient of my involvement as scoutmaster, baseball manager, ski patroller, soccer fan, etc. He's the one that gave me the last opportunity to be what I should have been to his brothers and sister. I don't think this extra time spent with Ron made me a better father necessarily, and it certainly did not make his two older brothers less of sons, but of course it had to make some difference. For instance, he is the only one of my sons that asks me for advice. The occasional phone calls or conversations that include the question, "Dad, what do you think about......?" are warmly gratifying. I see a little bit of me in his choice of vocation, human relations, and decision making in life. Ron's siblings are so terrific, that all credit must go to their mother. The results would indicate that the father's role is the same whether it is reactive or proactive, but I think not. We all live our lives with some regrets; my regret is that I did not take a more active role as a father to all my children. Memories are so priceless. With Ron, I recall him accidentally stabbing his face while throwing a temper tantrum, excelling in Kung-Fu, playing the drums, buying a dog

and eating his dinners by finishing one item at a time. Being ethnic Chinese, I was glad that he took some measure of interest in the Chinese culture and followed his brother's footsteps by serving as president of the Chinese Club in college. I'm proud of him now as a professional and as a new father. It is said that fathers live through their sons. It is their link to immortality. I would be happy to live forever in my son's images.

Ron Lee: Though it seems like just yesterday, it's been a long time since Dad and I first played golf. He started me out with three irons, one wood and a lot of hours at the Tilden Park driving range. He introduced me to the game, and instructed me on the basics of swinging a club and hitting a golf ball. It was a teacher-student type of affair, and a lot of fun. Dad has always taken pride in how he teaches; he has a certain methodical way of teaching no matter what the situation. It must come from his parents, who were both educators. On the other hand, I was a lousy student, always thinking I knew what was correct and incorrect. I'm sure this is why I could never overcome the severe slice I had. Anyway, after a year or so of golfing together, for whatever reason, we both stopped playing. We did other things together, just not golf.

Within the last year, a couple of significant things have happened. First, my wife and I had our first child, Mitchell. Second, Dad and I started playing golf together again.

Dad and I usually walk the golf course. It gives us the chance to talk about a lot of things. We occasionally talk about Mitchell, his future, and golf. We talk about the printing industry, since we both started small businesses there. But, most of the time we just shoot the breeze, talking about everything unimportant. The first time we did this, it amazed me; it is so uncharacteristic for Dad and I to talk about nothing. I look forward to each time we can get out and play...and talk about nothing at all, one-on-one, father-to-father.

Mitchell and I have mostly one-sided conversations now, although it is quickly becoming a dialogue. Every step in his development gets better than the one before. It's exciting to know that we'll be going through all of this together. It's hard to say what kind of relationship we'll have; I just feel lucky to have such a great little guy as my son. Mitchell and golfing with my dad are separately great things, how one affects the other makes each one better. Since Mitchell's arrival, I can say there aren't many things better than being a father, except maybe being a son.

Rowland Pringle, *Retired Marketing Supervisor*
David Pringle, *Physical Therapist*

David Pringle: I vividly recall one 4th of July weekend pleading with dad to see a fireworks display with some rather questionable company. As a wise and mature eleven year old, I couldn't comprehend any reason any parent would deny my request. My father, of course, felt otherwise. Conflict quickly ensued and harsh words were said. In an effort to reconcile our difference of opinion, my dad offered me his companionship by proposing a fishing trip instead. I was quick to decline his offer, and eventually convinced him to let me go to the fireworks display. The fireworks outing was so uneventful that I recall more about the struggle to go than the outing itself.

This seemingly trivial conflict had no significance until I was twenty years old. There I sat in my college apartment remembering how I had rejected, not just an outing with my dad, but his love as well. How badly he must have felt, and how callous I had been.

It became clear to me then that my dad really did love me. I wasn't completely sure of his love, until that day in my college apartment. When I was a child, my father was so driven by work, involvement in social clubs and various projects, that I didn't experience his love as he may have intended. I was not the child that ran to Daddy when he came home. I was the child at a distance who hoped his father wasn't grumpy and tired.

This all changed when I was twelve years old. Dad suddenly developed a much happier disposition. His time spent at home increased, and there was more time for me as a result. Eight years later, I finally recognized this.

It all makes sense now, as I look back. You see, when I was twelve, my father committed his life to Christ, and in return, he was a changed man. Eight years later, I did the same and began to comprehend how I had misunderstood my father. I now see my father differently and deeply appreciate who he is. He is no longer just my dad, but a special friend, whom I love very much.

Kae Saepharn, *Bilingual Instructional Assistant*
Jonathan Saepharn

Kae Saepharn: My son is very important to me, and we have a close relationship. We do many things together, but our favorite activity is fishing. We go all the time. I have taught my son many things, but the most important ones are to pursue his education, to respect his elders and teachers, and to not forget his culture. I am sure that I will be proud of my son no matter what he chooses to do with his life, but my dream is that he will become the first Mien doctor. That would make me especially proud.

" I have taught my son many things, but the most important ones are to pursue his education, to respect his elders and teachers, and to not forget his culture."

James Lewis Heller, *Printer*
James Lewis Heller, Jr.

James Heller: When we first adopted our children (they were three and four years old at the time), it was hard for me to adjust to having other people taking up my time. In fact, I even felt some resentment towards them for taking up so much of my time. Now, I don't see how I could have possibly ever felt that way. They are the ones I want to be with now. As time goes on, I am trying to be a better father by becoming more involved in my sons' life. I am very proud of my son, especially the progress he has made on his soccer team this year. I love my son as if he were my own, and in a way he is. As I grow as a father, and my son grows to be a man, our relationship is becoming something special. I wouldn't have things any other way.

"Does Father Always Know Best?", by Tony Wagner

Reading aloud and roughhousing are two of my favorite ways of being with my children. I don't remember my father roughhousing with us, though there's a picture of him with me on his shoulders in the family album. He never read to us. But he was a product of his time. Bill Cosby has made fathering more socially acceptable.

Reading aloud at bedtime has been my way of being a different kind of father. I began the routine when they were very young. For the longest time the books we read were dumb and I didn't enjoy reading them. But I liked the feeling of a child cuddling close and warm in my lap. And I couldn't wait for them to get older so we could read some good stuff together.

The Winnie-the-Pooh stories were fun for the language, and the real-life adventures of Laura Ingalls Wilder on the frontier were interesting, too. But it was "The Chronicles of Narnia," the seven-volume series by C. S. Lewis, that I've enjoyed reading aloud. The children always triumph in the end, but only with lots of help from their Narnian friends and by struggling to become more courageous and more generous.

I've nearly finished the sixth book with Eliza, one more to go, and already I'm beginning to feel a little sad. Eliza and I rarely roughhouse now. She's getting too old for it, and perhaps I am too. I get home much later than I used to and I'm more tired. And I confess that I like to play tennis on weekends. So I have this sense that when we finish the last "Narnia" book, a chapter in our lives will be over and I don't know what we'll share next.

But maybe I worry too much. I went in to say goodnight to Daniel, my oldest, the other night and we had a long chat about life, as we often do.

Then he asked me to stay and read to him. Daniel's fifteen now-we hadn't read aloud together in years. I stretched out next to him on the bed, which was barely big enough for the two of us, and began reading from a book he handed me. It was *The Odyssey*-his English class homework.

Together we read the second-to-last chapter, where Odysseus-adventurer, loyal husband and father-finally comes home a hero.

Would that I were he.

But I am not. I am my father's son-more involved with my children than he was, but, like him, offering love with strings attached: "If you stop pouting, Eliza, and if you hurry up with your ice cream and put your bowl in the dishwasher, then I'll read to you." Always the big "If," the list of things to be done first.

Must a father's love be earned? Perhaps my son will be a better father.

Gary Plummer: Grant, Garrett and I enjoy a lot of activities together. We have a nice, big backyard that we play football, baseball and basketball in. We also love to play video games. I enjoy spending time with my family, which is one of the reasons that I love being a professional athlete. One of the great things about it is that as a professional football player I get seven months off per year. Many people assume that being a professional athlete, that you are away from home a lot and not with your children. But, until the time I joined the 49ers, my kids were only fifteen minutes away. They would come to the training camp every day. We would wrestle after practice out on the field and have dinner together every evening. During football season the team is gone three days a week on ten different occasions. We leave for an away game on Friday and return on Sunday. The rest of the time we're home.

One thing Grant and Garrett get very excited about, as I do myself, is collecting sports memorabilia. They understand that it is something special to be able to have jerseys and helmets autographed by Jerry Rice, Steve Young, Barry Sanders, Emmett Smith and Deion Sanders in their bedroom. A lot of parents relive their childhood through their kids. They try and push their children to excel in sports or some other area. I haven't done that. In fact, I am not really concerned if they succeed in sports or not. The one way that I am reliving my childhood through my children is by collecting memorabilia with them. In fact, when I was a kid I always wanted to have one of every helmet in the league, which was only twenty-four teams and has now grown to thirty. We now have every helmet from every team in the league.

I talk to a lot of people about parenting and its importance in children's lives. A lot of people raise their kids with the attitude that whatever happens, happens and that they really have no control over the way that their children turn out. That attitude can be disastrous. I believe that as parents, we have to be proactive in our children's upbringing. Many people in sports have the attitude that they don't want to be looked at as a role model for kids, but I believe being a professional athlete is my opportunity to be a positive role model for children. It is a wonderful opportunity for someone in my position to demonstrate to kids what the right way to lead your life is.

Timothy Jemmott: In spite of all the talk about who should be our children's role models, I believe it is parents who are the real role models. It is our responsibility to teach our sons how to become productive men in our society. We need to teach our children morality, integrity, honesty and truthfulness, so they can grow up and truly be a blessing in our world. As a father, it is my responsibility to provide a conducive environment for that type of learning and growth to take place.

My own upbringing was developed more by observing my father, rather than by receiving direct instruction from him. That was partly because I grew up in a large family and he was spread pretty thin. When he was around, he was either sleeping, getting ready for the next job, or preoccupied with some other activity. He was a good role model, though. He always worked, he always provided and he was always there. When I look back, I say to myself, "How did he raise ten kids?" I have two and it's a huge responsibility, so I can't even imagine how he managed with ten. Now that I understand the challenges he faced, I respect him a lot more.

I believe that my children are a gift from the Lord. He gave them to my wife and me for now, but they still belong to Him. He's just giving us the opportunity to raise them. Just like Bill Cosby said about his son, we just thank God for having this time to enjoy them. While they are in my care, it is my job to give them a firm foundation, so they can use that foundation to do whatever God asks of them. I don't want to tell them what to do with their lives, but I do want to give them the tools, so as they get older, they can make decisions with intelligence and wisdom. That's my responsibility; to prepare them, to bring them up in the way they should go, so when they leave my home, they will be all right.

Jesus Rivera: There is an enormous difference in the personalities of my father, my son and myself. My father was very shy, I am very personable, and Hector has a very strong personality. Though we are very different, I still feel very close to my son. I spend a good deal of time talking to Hector. I give him advice, I hug him, and I tell him everything that I love about him. I also tell him about when I was a little boy, living in a miserable little poverty-stricken town where we scarcely had enough to eat. I am so glad that I have been able to give my son a better childhood than my own.

Hector Rivera: There are many things I love about my father. He tells me jokes a lot and it makes me laugh because he is really funny. He taught me how to ride my bike. I got mad though, because he made me crash. He plays video games with me, even though he isn't very good. My dad even gives me an allowance when I don't do anything all week.

" I spend a good deal of time talking to Hector. I give him advice, I hug him, and I tell him everything that I love about him."

Gary Costamagna: My wife and I have always tried to let the boys follow whatever they've decided to do. If they wanted to play Little League, I was the Little League coach. If they wanted to play soccer, I was the soccer coach and mom was the team mother. If they wanted to go skiing, we all put on skis and headed for the snow.

Chris was away at college when he told me he wanted to try going into the fire academy. He knew what the inside of a fire station was like, but he never hung out there. Family visits were always pretty short, on holidays or weekends. I don't think Chris decided he wanted to be a firefighter until he reached college, but we talked about it and I let him know I supported his decision. I think it's important to give your children the freedom to make their own choices. But, I have to admit, I am proud that Chris wanted to follow in my footsteps.

Chris Costamagna: When I graduated from the Sacramento Fire Academy, my dad, as fire chief, had to pin my badge on. I still get choked up when I talk about it. I was the seventh person to receive my badge on stage, so the moment was just building and building. Finally, when I went up there, he leaned over and whispered, "Are you as nervous as I am?" I said, "Yeah."

Dad was so nervous that he was fumbling with the pin. I remember he had a difficult time getting the badge on. It seemed like hours went by while he was pinning the badge on my uniform. He was getting tears in his eyes. I was too. When he finally got the badge on, he went to shake my hand which is (I don't know if he knows this) typical of our relationship because we usually shake hands instead of hug. But this was different. Simultaneously, we both went from shaking hands to hugging. I remember he squeezed me so hard, I gave this little squeak of a cry. It was a very emotional time for both of us. After I got my badge, I had to shake hands with the other chiefs and captains in the line-up. I couldn't look at any of them. I didn't want them to see I had tears in my eyes. I just wanted to get off the stage and sit down.

One of the reasons the graduation was so emotional is because my father pinned his first badge on me. It's neat because the badge is number 277 and everybody in my graduating class has a number in the high 700s. Also, the older badges say "fireman" instead of "firefighter." Some people don't think I'm deserving of the badge, because I wasn't brought up in the era of the "fireman." I'm a firefighter. Only the veteran firefighters in the department have this kind of a badge. But just the fact that it was my dad's badge makes most people accept it.

Kids today have people like Michael Jordan and other sports figures, or TV people that they look up to, but I've always looked up to my dad. He is my hero and my idol. There's just nobody that stands taller in my eyes than my father.

70

Pedro Adams, Jr., *Ocularist*
Pedro Anthony Adams

Pedro Adams, Jr.: I want to give Pete a life with meaning. At fifty-one, I'm not young. It's not that I'm old or anything, but it's just that I want to give him as much knowledge as I can. Pete and I have become buddies. I have always been waiting for that. When are we going to become buddies? When is that bond going to happen? It was already happening without my realizing it. Before I knew it, I was his hero.

Whenever I am doing something, I usually have Pete come along. We go places together or we fix something like the lawn mower. He hands me the screwdriver. We do it together, Pete and me. We're never in a hurry. It just takes two to three times longer to do anything. It's just a pleasure introducing him to new things for the first time.

My father was my idol, my hero. I think what I'm doing now is what my father did for me.

Pedro Adams: My dad's great; he's my friend. We'll always be buddies. I went fishing with my dad. He only caught one fish, one small fish, and I caught five big ones. He had a blue hat and I had a red hat and we were racing and I had the most fish. All the fish came to me because I was being totally still, and my dad was moving around. He was trying to teach me how to fish and I already knew. He only caught one small fish.

*" Before I knew it,
I was his hero."*

Sam Kipp, *Retired College Educator/Photographer*
Joe Kipp, *Photographer*

Sam Kipp: We have a very warm, friendly father-son relationship. We share an interest in photography. I try to curb my enthusiasm, but out of five children, Joe's the only one doing photography. Joe is a very kind and considerate person. He's very, very thoughtful. For example, when I ask him to do something for me that I can't do around the house anymore, he's usually already done it.

Joe Kipp: I appreciate the importance of imagery in life. To see what somebody enjoys photographing is interesting. It's not a verbal expression, but it certainly communicates who a person is. It's a vital form of communication for me. I am not one who talks a great deal. I don't know that my father and I have had any long conversations, so imagery has been an open and very real form of communication between the two of us.

My dad is caring, in a big way. He likes to help people and see them do well. He allows people to have room and make mistakes, without building any walls that would make you feel you cannot return. Growing up, we had the usual conflicts. Our ideas would clash head on. We grew up in different times, but over the past years, we've come together as friends. I think photography has been a means of our coming to terms with our relationship.

Arturo Venegas: I am committed to helping my kids achieve their dreams. I have always felt that my children are destined to achieve far greater things than I have ever dreamed of. However, the only thing I have expected of them is that they turn out to be good, decent people. I want them to recognize that there are people less fortunate than they, and that it is up to them to help improve their lot. This world can be a better place, if they will contribute to it. Recently, I got to take them back to Mexico and show them where I was born. That was really important to me. It gave them the perspective that they truly have the ability to succeed. You see, if I could come from there, to where I am now, then given the opportunities available in this country, they have the potential to achieve much greater things than I have. It was important for them to see this with their own eyes.

Anthony Venegas: I would really like to fly. Being the first man on Mars would be cool. I plan on going to the Air Force first, and then onto NASA.

Andrew Venegas: When I grow up I want to be a prosecutor, and eventually a judge.

Paul Thick, *Graphic Designer*
Trevor Thick

Paul Thick: I have a few memories of my son Trevor that stand out above the rest. The first is when he was about nine months old. I was sitting on the couch holding and rocking him. Soon, he put his head down on my shoulder and fell peacefully asleep. I think I sat there for two more hours enjoying the feelings of closeness, security and love. He is now three and it's practically impossible to get him to sit still for more than ten seconds.

Another fond memory I have of Trevor is our first garden together in our new house. Trevor was two and I had just prepared the soil when he came out to help. We selected seeds to plant-some peas, beans, radishes and carrots. I would poke a hole in the ground and give Trevor a seed. He would drop it in, cover it with dirt and pat it down. His favorite part was the patting. We spent hours doing this and kept track of our plants all summer.

So far, I think I'm doing fine as a father. Though I find myself having to work a lot and not being able to spend as much time with him as I would like. In raising Trevor, I am trying not to make the same mistakes that my father did. I never felt I could go to my father to talk about anything that was important. I want to make sure our relationship stays close enough that Trevor knows he can come and talk to me anytime. I'm sure the future holds many more wonderful memories for Trevor and me and I look forward to every one.

Congressman Robert Matsui, *U.S. Congressman*
Brian Matsui, *Student, Stanford University Law School*

Robert Matsui: Brian was a really great kid, and has matured into a sensitive, yet determined individual. He was our only child, so he was, to a great degree, the focus of our lives. For my parents, he was the only grandchild. I was very close to my father. In fact, I had to pull out of the Senate race because I wanted to spend time with him before he died. Brian was a great help to me during that time. During June and July of 1991, he stayed with his grandfather. My father died on August 1, 1991. I don't think Brian realized how important his being there was. He and my father bonded by nature. They were so close.

Brian was a big collector of baseball cards. When I was a kid I collected them as well. One day a couple of lobbyists came in to see me. One of the lobbyists (Evan Tisdale) saw that I had some of Brian's baseball cards in my cabinet. They weren't worth very much, five dollars each or something of that nature. Well, he saw those baseball cards, and asked if I collected them. I told him no, but my son did and that he had given them to me, so I had decided to put them up. A few days later Evan came by and gave me an envelope with about 15 baseball cards. The cards went all the way back to 1953 or 1954, with names like Jackie Robinson and Duke Snyder. I said, "My God, these cards are fantastic!" So I brought them home and gave them to Brian, who was in high school at the time. He took them up to his room and came back in a little while and said, "Dad, do you want to go to jail?" I said, "What do you mean?" "Dad, these cards are worth a lot of money. Don't you have a gift limit?" "Sure I do. I think it's around $200." "Well," he said, "You can't take these cards, or you might go to jail!" The next day, I called Evan and asked him to come by the office. I said, "Evan, I'm sorry, but I have to give those baseball cards back to you." Evan said, "Bob, but those were just for fun." "I know Evan, but my son and I just had a little lesson in morality."

Well, Evan took the cards back, but the funny thing was, that he told a couple of folks about what happened and CNN and ABC picked up the story and the next thing we knew they wanted to interview Brian and me. They did this interview at our house with Brian and me looking at the baseball cards with the voice-over talking about limitations on members of Congress accepting gifts. Later that night, during dinner, Brian said, "You know, I should have never done that interview. Dad, can you imagine when I go to school tomorrow? I mean, only nerds who are my age collect baseball cards."

I'll never forget that.

80

Fred Masteller, *Retired Minister*
J.R. Masteller, *Christian School Administrator*

Fred Masteller: I remember when J.R. was a senior in high school, and I had given him permission to drive my car on a short trip into town. On the way, he took his eyes off the road for a second, the car in front of him stopped, he plowed into it and the car that was following plowed into him. It was a three car accident with my car totaled. When he was driven home by the police that afternoon, it was very difficult for him to break the news that he totaled Dad's car. When he told me the news, I asked him two questions: "Was anyone hurt?" "No Dad, but your car is totaled." I replied, "Son, you can always replace metal and glass, but never flesh and blood." Immediately I could see the relief come to his face. Then I asked, "was she pretty?" He knew that I had already figured out that it was a girl that had caused him to take his eyes off the road for a second. He laughed and said, "Yes dad, she was." I wasn't that upset, because I believed that he had wrecked God's car, and not mine. It was up to God to replace the car. To make a long story short, God not only replaced that car, but we ended up $800 in the black. I have great memories of a great son.

Several years ago, I had the privilege of ordaining my son into the Christian ministry. He was thirty-four at the time. One thing he said when he was asking me to ordain him was, "Dad, it takes some a little longer than others to grow up." I am proud of my son and I love him very much. He is the Vice-Principal of a growing Christian school and someday very soon he will be the Principal. The staff and students think highly of him, but no one thinks higher of him than his Dad.....

J.R. Masteller: My dad and I both love music and we sing with tremendous emotion. It's hard for us to hold back the tears when we sing. We both love to scream at a T.V. ball game when the officials have blown a call (even during the instant replay!). We both love to give and receive hugs, and have a deep longing to be affirmed by others. We both are extremely competitive in sports and games. We also relish an afternoon nap!

Dad has been a church pastor/evangelist all his Christian life, and I am in ministry as a Christian School Administrator. Although Dad made it clear that his dream was that I follow in his footsteps in the pulpit ministry, he always stated that he would be proud of me in anything I chose to do, so long as it was God-directed. There has never been any question in my mind that Dad loves God first, mom second and his family third. I am glad to say that I have inherited that quality from him.

My father always taught me, through his words and his actions, to have my priorities in the right order. Above all, Dad taught me to be a man of prayer. This was the subject of his charge at my ordination into the ministry. A man of prayer will have his priorities in the proper order.

I consider dad my best friend now, but that has only come recently. I have come to realize that he is, and has always been, my biggest fan. He has been praying for me for many, many years. Through many sorrows and heartaches, he has always been the one to champion my cause. I love my Dad.

Michael Rabadam, *Desktop Publishing*
Carlo Rabadam

Michael Rabadam: My son, Carlo, is five years old. Sunday and Monday are my days off, so Monday has always been a very special day for my son and me. For five years we have spent it together while my wife has been at work and my daughter at school.

I remember when Carlo was born. The entire procedure of the Caesarean section is still very clear in my mind. From the time the nurse offered me a scrub gown, to the incision, and finally the doctor scooping him out of my wife's belly. I saw his eyes open wide and I cut the umbilical cord. He was a big baby, almost nine pounds.

Since he will start kindergarten in the fall, my son and I won't have Mondays to ourselves anymore. However, I look forward to guiding him through the magical window of learning.

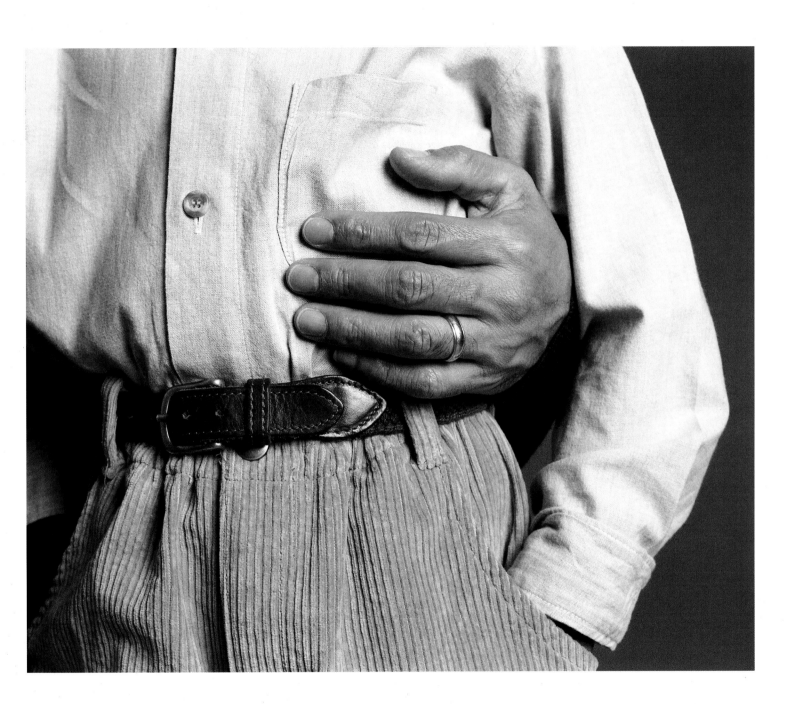

Dugan Aguilar, *Graphic Artist/Photographer*
Dustin Aguilar, *Student*

Dugan Aguilar: When Dustin was born, there were no words to describe my feelings; maybe euphoria would be one. I went home and called everyone to let them know that I had a son! My wife and I worked different shifts, so I was able to spend a great deal of time and really bond with Dustin. It was just Dustin and me in the mornings, so I was doing everything from feeding and changing him, to watching "Sesame Street" with him. We also listened to music. This is the common denominator between my father, myself and my son; we all listen to music. Dustin has a thing about buying CDs. I tell him not to buy as many as he does, and then I wonder if I should step back and look at my old record album collection. I know that I need to give him more room for growth and not be so domineering. I'm the opposite of my father, who gave me a lot of leeway. Because I work swing shift, I have missed a lot of time with my son. I need to find time to be with him and do things with him. It is hard to balance everything. Time is very precious, and we must use it wisely. One thing that I would like to pass on to my son is the need take a particular talent and work hard at it and don't quit. Quitting is too easy of a way out. This was a very important lesson that I learned from my father; he never missed a day of work. I love my father and have tried to please him and make him proud of me. I have done things in my life, some good and some bad, but he always forgives the bad. My son is very affectionate and I'm lucky to have him, and I know he will grow up to be a fine person.

Dustin Aguilar: My father and I have not always had a good relationship. We fight a lot about very trivial issues. I guess neither of us ever wants to admit that we are wrong. I've never really felt very close to my father. We haven't really spent a lot of time together since I was a little kid. I think we only spend time together once a month. I wish it could be more. I always wish that we could have been closer. Sometimes I feel like I barely have a dad. I feel very isolated from him and the distance we have built up makes me feel very sad and alone. My dad has always worked nights so I only see him during the weekend. I am a very busy person and that causes us to see each other even less.

I think many different factors affect our relationship. Our different interests make it difficult for us to be together and get along. He tries to tell me what I can spend my money on and he hints at the stuff I wear or do that he doesn't like...I wish he would just tell me or not tell me. I don't think he wants to give me very much freedom.

Although it's not always a great relationship, I always love the time we do get to spend together. It's hard to have a good relationship when you're a teenager with your parents, but in spite of our problems, I still love my dad.

Ray Solone, *Advertising Agency Owner*
Mitchell Solone

Ray Solone: Fatherhood. It means so many things to so many people. To me it means an opportunity and a commitment to shape, influence and create a personality that most reflects my own, my father's, my heroes' and my *dreams.* My father's goal in life was to provide for his family the best that he could and to hope that his children would create a life for themselves that was better than his own. My goal is to deliver every opportunity at my disposal to my son so that he can enjoy life to its fullest and to contribute to our society while doing so. While I write it, it seems like any father's goal. When I ponder it, it seems somewhat overwhelming. As I live it, we'll see how it changes.

Charles Meng: Debby and I wanted to have a family from the day we started talking marriage. After we married, we assumed that when we wished to conceive, we would. However, we soon found out that we might not ever be able to have children. We spent the next two years undergoing numerous tests and procedures. Finally, at the end of the second year, my son Christian was conceived! My wife went through twenty hours of labor and then had to endure a caesarean operation. I was so overjoyed when Christian was born that I reached over and tried to hold him immediately! The day he was born, October 12, was a very special day for us because it was the anniversary of our marriage. From the very day we knew we were having a boy, I started telling him that I loved him. Every night since Christian has blessed our lives, I have crept into his room and whispered, "Daddy loves you, Christian!" I also spend time, daily, playing and reading to him. I can tell you after waiting for thirty-five years to be a father, I understand what love is between a father and a son. I want my son to know how important it is to tell your children that you love them every day and to spend time with them. The time you spend with your child reinforces what you say.

" I can tell you after waiting for thirty-five years to be a father, I understand what love is between a father and a son."

A letter from President Theodore Roosevelt to his son Kermit.

Dear Kermit,

I was very glad to get your letter. Am glad you are playing football. I should be very sorry to see either you or Ted devoting most of your attention to athletics, and I haven't got any special ambition to see you shine overmuch in athletics at college, at least (if you go there), because I think it tends to take up too much time; but I do like to feel that you are manly and able to hold your own in rough, hardy sports. I would rather have a boy of mine stand high in his studies than high in athletics, but I could a great deal rather have him show true manliness of character than show either intellectual or physical prowess; and I believe you and Ted both bid fair to develop just such character.

There! you will think this a dreadfully preaching letter! I suppose I have a natural tendency to preach just at present because I am overwhelmed with my work. I enjoy being President, and I like to do the work and have my hand on the lever. But it is very worrying and puzzling, and I have to make up my mind to accept every kind of attack and misrepresentation. It is a great comfort to me to read the life and letters of Abraham Lincoln. I am more and more impressed every day, not only with the man's wonderful power and sagacity, but with his literally endless patience, and at the same time his unflinching resolution.

your loving father

Louie González: When I was three or four years old, I remember waiting for my father, "mi 'apa", to arrive home from work so that I could sit on his lap and pull on his ear. I do not know what it was about this simple act, but it used to make me laugh. While he and my mother, "mi 'ama" would exchange "cuentos" (stories) about the day's events, I would listen closely in order to be the first one to know which one of my siblings was "in for it." My father preferred to give us "consejos" (advice), rather than discipline us, whereas my mother would insist on a more traditional approach after having dealt with us all day.

Jose González Valle, my father, worked honorably all of his life and encouraged his children to pursue their education and to have pride in their Mexican heritage and culture. "After all," he would say, "this was Mexico long before it was the United States and it will continue to be so, in spirit, until the end of time." "Mi'apa" created music in the early hours of the morning and did not even know it; the percolating water in the coffee pot, the ringing of the spoon against the sides of his cup, and the rhythm of the water splashing against the rosales (rosebushes) outside as he waited for his ride to work.

My sons, Jose Luis and Andres, are eighteen months apart in age. Their personalities are somewhat different, but they share too many things in common not to be good friends. They have matured with a wonderful sense of humor and a profound respect for all living things. Jose Luis plays his Fender Stratt guitar better than I ever will, and I truly enjoy hearing him play. Andres is usually the first to start laughing and enticing everyone to join in. He likes to add a little style to everything he does.

I trust Jose Luis and Andres completely and I know that they have faith in my desire to do what is best for them and their future. I would like them to find significance in many things-in the importance of dreams, in the incorporation of independence into their daily lives, in books and movies, in having breakfast together at Eddie's, in printing huelga flags for Cesar Chavez, and in resisting racism and bigotry.

As an artist, there are times when inspiration has no schedule. To be honest to the expression, one needs to spend the time no matter how exhausting it is. For this I want to thank "mis hijos" for allowing me to have the time to be a creative person. Every piece of art that is born in my studio, contains a part of their immense generosity in its essence.

Jose Luis González: "Mom" I said, "Can Dean come over so we can go to the mall or something later on this evening?" She hesitated. "Well let me think about it." Fifteen minutes later, a knock on the door aroused my mother's curiosity. "Who could that be?", she asked. As she opened the door and the anxious eyes of Dean glared into the dimly lit living room, my mother said, "Oh. Hi Dean. How are you?" "I'm okay," he replied. A few minutes later, my mom told me that she does not think that it is such a good idea for me to go out on a Friday night. This struck me as odd, because my usual Friday night consists of going out on the town with my friends. She was mad because I did not wait for her consent for Dean to come over. Then Big Lou came to my defense and tried to make her see that it was not such a big deal. He argued that, "Dean comes over every Friday. I've actually been expecting him to show up." Later that night, I was having a great time bowling with some of my friends. I got home about ten o'clock in the evening, which is earlier than my usual arrival time.

My father, brother, and I are on a team. The opposing force is my mom. We battle many things, including everyday nagging and requests. We endure this with the jokes (usually about her) that we share. All in all though, we love her very much. My father and I share a very important thing, trust. You need it to live. I hope that we live for a very long time.

Andres González: One thing that I like about my father, is that although he does not like basketball very much, he enjoys going to my games. When I was very little, I enjoyed wrestling with my dad and my brother. "Foot" used to get us in head locks and we were "stuck like Chuck." What I like now is that almost every Saturday my brother, dad, and I go to Eddie's for breakfast. I usually get two eggs, bacon, and fried rice.

Kim Steele: I remember being pushed by my father to succeed in sports, which was something that could be good and bad for a young boy. My father played baseball with me and taught me all facets of the game. He inspired me to be driven to excel in athletics, or anything else I undertook. I remember my father as a powerful influence in my life. He was a strong-willed father whose anger I both feared and respected.

My son and I have enjoyed some of the same things my father and I enjoyed together: fishing, camping, lizard hunting and the appreciation of nature. We have also been involved with Scouting and created Pinewood Derby Cars. My son received his first trophy at the age of eight for his entry of a car in the Pinewood Derby competition. I also won my first trophy at the age of eight, but mine was for first place in a baseball league.

Timmy and I are alike and different in quite a few ways. My son is more compassionate and accepting of children with special challenges than I was at his age. He has not been pushed to be involved in sports, nor groomed to be one who excels in baseball, football, or basketball (as I was). But, he has recently blossomed physically and shows signs of natural athletic skills. Timmy has artistic abilities that I did not try to develop when I was his age. My son is still in a stage of innocence. I believe this next year will be a time for my son, where some of the innocence of childhood will give way to the realities of growing up and peer pressure. I have always tucked my kids into bed and kissed them good night, so I believe this and other personal involvement has kept us close. The best years are yet to come, as I have the opportunity to watch Timmy mature and develop into a young man. I pray that I may draw near to God and bring my kids near with me.

Tim Steele: I like to spend time with my dad. I like to wrestle and play golf with him. I also like to catch frogs, lizards, and snakes with him. I like to read with him, but sometimes he reads too much. I wish he didn't have to work so much and could be home more. He taught me how to use a bow and arrow and how to use a pocket knife. My Dad is a lot of fun!

Pat Martin: There has always been something special about my son. I'm sure all parents have these same feelings for their kids. But from the second he was born, there was something about Denver that we just couldn't put our finger on. Maybe it's because he is a truly good soul. I can't remember when Denver and I started really communicating, but ever since that time we have been best friends. Not like the way my wife and I are best friends, but in a way only a father and son can be. When Denver was two years old something happened to him that would change our lives profoundly. He was diagnosed with Leukemia.

The first year of chemotherapy was painful and traumatic, but through it all he handled those difficult times with strength, courage, and a maturity beyond his years. It's funny, I don't think my wife or I ever doubted for a moment that Denver would make it through okay. It's just the kind of person he is. Three and a half years after being diagnosed my son received his last treatment, and at the time of this writing, is in complete remission. His chances for a total recovery are considered excellent. It was during this ordeal that we became especially close, although I would like to think we'd be just as close if nothing had ever happened. I guess we'll never know. One thing's for sure, I have always admired Denver's capacity to deal with whatever situation comes his way. One day we were walking along the railroad tracks near our house. We were crossing a bridge that went over a road when out of nowhere a speeding train came upon us. Running for our lives, we jumped off the bridge. As we landed and turned to look, it seemed that half the train had already passed by. Denver looked at me and said, "That was pretty close, huh Dad?" We both started laughing. The whole thing was right out of the train scene in the movie "Stand By Me." We still talk about that day. I can't believe how lucky I am to have such a wonderful son. He truly is something special.

Tony Harris: I believe that my main job as a father is to show love. Love is the key in my household. It's very important that my kids and my wife understand how much I truly love them and really feel they are a blessing to me. My second job is to provide my children with moral and spiritual guidance and education. I spend a lot of time just talking with my son. My goal for my son, is that he will grow up to be a good Christian and a benefit to our society. I try to accomplish that by setting an example, and by taking time to be with him and to teach him. It's so easy now to get too busy, and before you know it, your children have grown up, and you didn't teach them all that you needed to. I really don't want to see that happen.

One of the things my son and I love to do is to go out on the first Sunday of the month and visit the sick. It's one way in which we serve our community. The sick and shut-ins that we have been visiting have enjoyed watching my son grow up over the last few years. They look forward to seeing him on our monthly visits. He really enjoys it, too.

In our society, today, I believe it is important to try and be a mentor to those young men who do not have a father. It is something that I have chosen to do, and I know it can make a difference. For example, I met a young man who was still in high school at the time, and didn't know where his life was going. We developed a relationship and I encouraged him to focus on his education and establish goals for his life. Now he's graduated from Berkeley with a degree in Architecture, and is currently attending Harvard University. I am so excited for this young man. It really didn't take much from me, except time. I just took a little time here and there to encourage him and push him in the right direction. He just took off on his own after that.

Colin Meyer, *Heavy Equipment Operator*
Michael Vernon Meyer, *Student*

Colin Meyer: To say Mike loves sports is the biggest understatement a person could make. Growing up he played baseball, football, tennis, golf, volleyball, and anything else that came along. If he wasn't playing sports, he was watching it on T.V. I was busy working two jobs so we didn't spend a lot of time together. We all enjoyed his years in Pop Warner football, and we were especially proud when in his last year he won the coveted Mr. Hardnose award.

Because he has been a sports fanatic since he was a toddler, it finally rubbed off on me. We now enjoy a good rivalry between his football team, the Pittsburgh Steelers, and mine, the San Francisco 49ers. We call often during the games just to needle each other.

It is since Mike has became an adult though, that we have grown really close. Growing up he wasn't very interested in what I was doing. I believe he is now trying to make up for lost time. He seems like a sponge soaking up all I can teach him, from learning how to work on his own vehicle, to doing his own household repairs. He always earned good grades in school and to this day strives to do better than his best.

I love my son, and he has made me very proud.

Michael Meyer: When I was young I can remember not relating to my father at all. My father was always working at one job or another. It seemed to me that he wanted to work rather than be at my sporting events, or play catch with me in the backyard. I guess that I resented my father for not being there when I wanted him to be. There were many times that I would look up and try to find my father watching me or cheering for me when I did something I thought was special. It took a long time for me to realize that my father was not working because he wanted to, but because he had to. I know now that the special moments that he missed were much more painful to him, than they were to me. As I have grown into a young man, I am able to understand how hard it is to balance your work and your personal life. The trick is to work as hard as you possibly can and at the same love as hard as you possibly can. I have learned this lesson from my father. I may not have learned how to throw a ball from my father, but I have learned how to provide for and love the people I care about. Each day that I grow older, I feel his personality and morals becoming my own. I have learned more about kindness and generosity from my father than any son has a right to learn. He has become my best friend as well as my hero. Not many people can love their hero the way I love my father. Thanks, Dad, for more than you know!

Jeoffrey Benward: I've heard it said that your children mirror many of the things you like and don't like about yourself. As Aaron grew, I saw many similarities between us. He loves sports, music, and he grew to love God. Early on in our relationship, I saw the importance of nurturing his weaknesses, which were few, and challenging his strengths. Knowing all along that his personality did act as a mirror of mine, I became sensitive to the fact that I should never react when I saw myself glaring back at me through my son.

My greatest success in raising Aaron is that he embraced Christ as his Savior and he's truly a compassionate man. I know I've failed at times not modeling the person of Christ to my kids. I regret the moments I was not the example Aaron needed to see. Aaron is teaching me by example that I don't have to be perfect. I struggle with perfectionism. I'm stressed, he's laid back. I need to get it done now, he knows there's time.

I heard early on in my mentoring process with Aaron, that the greatest gift we can give our children is the sensitivity to who they are. I've always been one who tries to read the moment. I love my son and I know he'll be a great father. I hope I've given him something he can pass on to his son, Luke Aaron. Yes, I'm a grandfather and I pray I'm a good one.

The results of a fatherless society are everywhere. Over the years I've had the privilege of ministering in prisons across the U.S. Without exception, 80% to 85% of the inmates come from fatherless homes. I think the pain speaks for itself. We need our dad.

Aaron Benward: Some of the greatest memories I have of my dad are from my basketball games in high school. To us, Tuesday and Friday evenings (game nights) were the biggest highlights of every week. I would come running out of the tunnel and without fail, I could look to the front row of the bleachers at half-court and see my dad cheering me on. There was nothing that could come between him and my game. Boy, would he work those referees over! Whether I had a great game or a not-so-great game, deep down what I valued most was that my dad was there

to encourage, support, and most of all, show me that he loved me. As a teenager, his commitment to being at my games was one of the many things that showed me that I, along with the rest of the family, was the most important thing in his life. No meeting, no job, no problem, no distance, no lack of sleep, was ever more important to my dad than coming to watch me play. As I look back at those times, I realize as a teenager who loved his dad, that it was the ultimate way for me to see how much of a priority I was to him.

Now that I'm twenty-three and working with my dad full-time, I consider it a treasure in my life. Yes, there are trying times but the good far outweighs the bad. I believe my father and I are reaping the benefits of those times spent at basketball games now in our ministry. What I mean is, the reason we have such an awesome relationship is because I know how much I mean to my dad. Our relationship just doesn't happen, though. We still have to work at it. We both have to serve each other by thinking of the other one first. We have our problems, quarrels, and other situations we must deal with from time to time. But, to look over on stage and see my Dad singing, brings all those memories back again.

Donovan Dilworth: Nathanael is so together for his age, I can't believe it. He is so outgoing, whereas Jonathan is very quiet, much like I am. Jonathan is always telling me that I'm his best friend. I tell them they are special, and that they're loved a lot, but I also let them know what their boundaries are. When they were born, I was ecstatic. I was so excited to have been given this gift. And they are gifts.

Nathanael Dilworth: He loves me and Jonathan most of all.

" When they were born, I was ecstatic. I was so excited to have been given this gift."

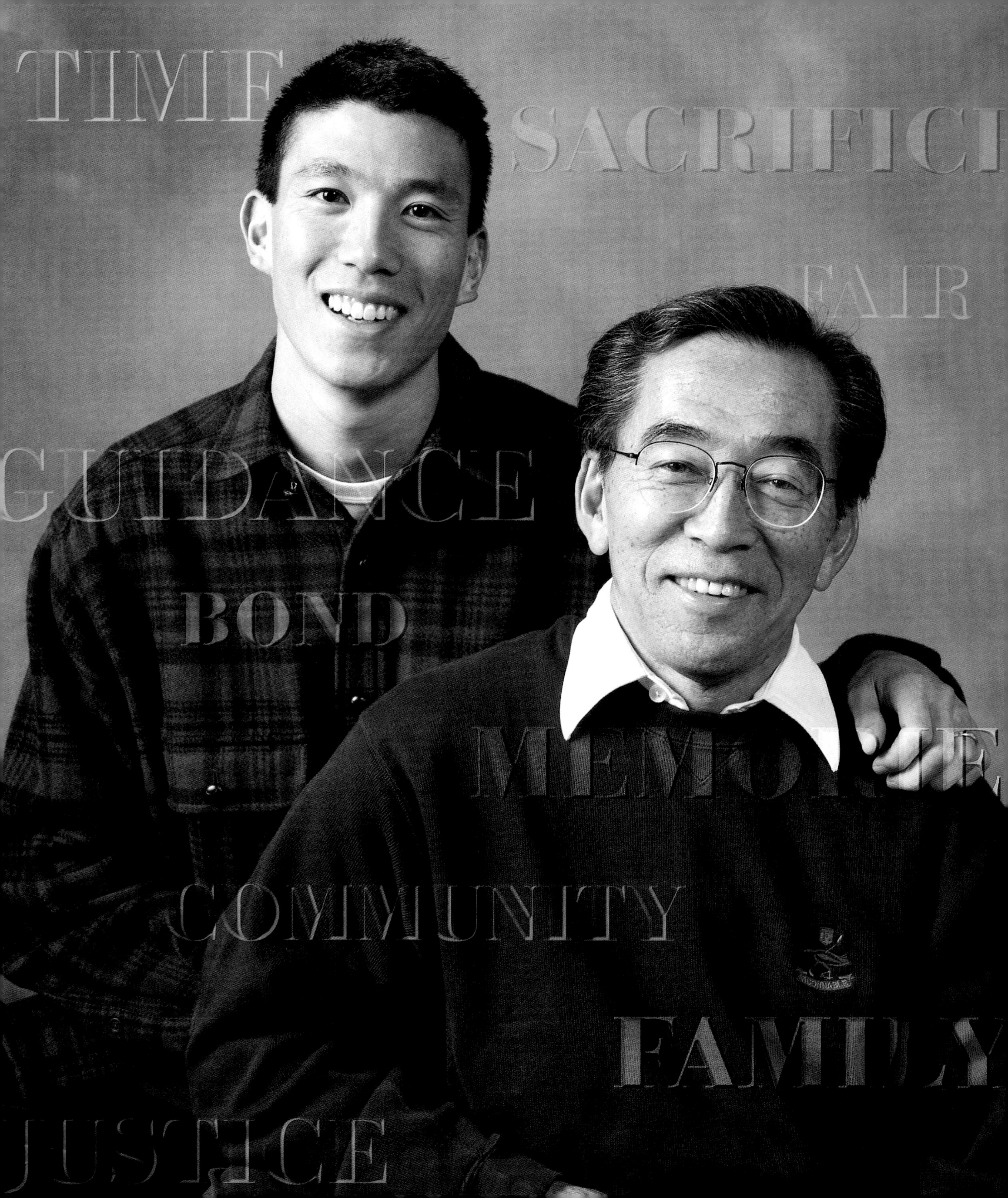
TIME
SACRIFICE
FAIR
GUIDANCE
BOND
COMMUNITY
FAMILY
JUSTICE

Charles Kobayashi: At one time I had a law practice. When my daughter was about four years old (around the time that my son was born), I gave up my practice and went to work for the District Attorney's Office. My decision was based on my desire to spend time with my family. Having your own practice requires a great deal of time, time that I decided should be spent raising my children. After working for the District Attorney's Office for seventeen years, I was appointed a judge. I deal with cases that involve family law.

My position has caused me to examine the difficulties that so many children encounter. I firmly believe that every child needs a mother and a father. Kids need guidance from their parents and they need role models. Children need to be taught values, and that they have a responsibility to their friends, their family, and their community. The mother and father also need to be participating in their childrens lives, encouraging them, disciplining them and guiding them in a positive manner.

My son and I did a lot of things together as he was growing up. We were involved in Indian Guides, Boy Scouts (he became an Eagle Scout), soccer, and Little League Baseball. Greg also became a very good tennis player. Our family traveled all over Northern California to his tennis tournaments on the weekends. He eventually played for St. Mary's College and was captain of his team for two years. My wife and I were also involved in many of our children's school activities. I think we were able to give our kids a lot, not monetarily, but through participation in their lives. My wife and I have a lot of great memories that are permanently etched in our minds and in our many photographs, and you can't buy those with money.

Greg Kobayashi: When I graduated from college, my father wrote a quotation in a card for me from Shakespeare's Hamlet, "To Thy Own Self Be True." It has stayed with me as I have tried to steer myself through my life. I believe my father has lived his life by this quote. He has always been true to himself, his family and the community he serves. I would consider him a family person, enjoying quiet moments at home or a family dinner while playing with his grandsons. He has always placed us at the top of his list. He is truly an unselfish person. He has always taken the time to comfort me when I fall or urge me to better myself. If you were to look at my father's career and life, it is amazing how an individual could overcome so many adversities. As a Japanese American child, not speaking any English, he learned quickly how to communicate and become part of the American culture. He overcame the internment of the relocation camps of World War II and the continuance of racism through college and the beginning of his professional career. He took on every challenge head first, never letting any setback deter his ambition to make a difference in the world. Now, he sits behind a bench making decisions that can alter a family's life together. My father is a Superior Court Judge for the family law section. I cannot think of a more qualified person to be making these important decisions. If you ask my father's peers what they think about my father, the word "fair" is always used to describe him. He takes it upon himself to make the best decision for the child in the family. He studies their cases by taking the time to understand each person's needs and problems. He brings his cases home to study them even more. It is not just a job for him, but his way to make a difference in his community. According to my mother, his favorite day of the week is adoption day. After dealing with divorces, spousal abuse and child custody cases, he is able to bring a couple in search of a child, together with a child in need of parents, and let them leave as a family. My parents first came to the Judge's chambers thirty-one years ago, and again four years later; my sister and I are both adopted. Maybe that makes him a better judge up there, or maybe it is because he understands that a family is not just birth, but a bond of love and moments of sharing, sacrifices and forgiveness.

My parents have always sacrificed to make my sister's and my life a little better than theirs. As a result, they have given us every opportunity and experience to better enhance our lives and futures. As a husband, I hope to bring these family values to my home. Though I am not a father yet, I look forward to the days I can spend with my children, teaching them the values and lessons my parents taught me. It was never the material objects they gave us, but the moments shared over dinner or the time spent together as a family. Those are the memories I cherish. My father always had time for me, and continues to make time for me when I need him most. I still ask his opinion on all matters, because I value his opinion and judgment.

People talk about role models, usually a sports figure or politician. Nobody ever seems to want to be like their parents these days. My father is my role model; I have tried to mirror his image. I hope I can follow in his footsteps as an individual and as a parent. He has the drive and passion one needs to succeed in his career, and the love and care to keep his family together. He is successful because he has earned the respect of his peers and the love of his family and friends. For my father, it has never been about the awards or plaques, but about doing what is morally correct and helping others in their time of need. My father is a humble person, never taking the credit for any of his accomplishments, but always giving credit to others. But this is my father being "true" to himself and the others that surround him.

"To Thy Own Self Be True."

Chris Combrink, *Business Owner*
Christopher "Dane" & Clayton Combrink

Chris Combrink: I think being a father, today, is one of the most important things a man can do, not only for himself and his child, but the community around him. Our country is in one of the biggest moral declines of all time, and part of the problem is that men, in general, don't want to take the responsibility of being a father. Being a father is more than just putting food on the table, it's taking the time to show your child what is right and what is wrong, and to always be respectful towards those around you. Being a father is teaching them the consequences that go along with bad actions and being grateful for all that you have while taking nothing for granted. In almost every major city, there are young kids turning to drugs and gangs, desperately trying to fill that male role model void because their fathers are not around. It's hard to imagine what this great country of ours would be like if every father took this responsibility seriously. It's funny, but I had never thought about any of this until the birth of my oldest son six years ago. Before my son was born, I lived a carefree life. The only responsibility I had was work, and even that was fun, considering I worked at a ski resort. In my heart, I always felt that I would be a good dad, I just wasn't sure about all the responsibility that came with it. I think the good Lord saw me coming, because my son came with a little more responsibility than the average newborn. You see, my son Dane, had a very difficult delivery, which resulted in total paralysis from the neck down.

My wife and I spent Dane's first five months of life by his side, in a neonatal intensive care unit, while doctors tried to figure out what was wrong with him. After five months, Dane was stable enough to come home, needing a ventilator twenty-four hours a day to keep him alive. We had to relocate from the mountains to the city so we could be close to the hospital in case of an emergency. The doctors told us that Dane's nerves had been severed, and that he would probably never have the ability to crawl, walk, or even eat for that matter. The first thing I learned was that the power of prayer was very real. I also believed that the good Lord was going to show me a miracle with my son. From the moment Dane came home from the hospital he began getting stronger and recovering much more rapidly than anyone expected. First his fingers and toes would wiggle a little. Later on it was his legs or an arm. The doctors would tell us it was only muscle spasms and not to get too excited. But we knew better. As the months progressed all of Dane's functions seemed to be coming back fully. The last nerves to come back where his phrenic nerves, which controlled his diaphragm. After these nerves came back completely, Dane started weaning himself off the ventilator, until he no longer needed it while he was awake. The doctors now tell us that he will probably need the ventilator while he sleeps for the rest of his life. I have faith that Dane will one day be completely free of the machines that keep him alive. Both of my sons teach me new things about life every day while I try and raise them to the best of my ability. There are many things in this world that were never intended to be easy. Being a father is one of them. I guess that's why I feel it's so rewarding.

118

Dr. William Lee, *Publisher, The Observer Newspaper*
William Lee, Jr., *General Manager, The Observer Newspaper*
Larry Lee, *Director, Technical Production, The Observer Newspaper*

Dr. William Lee: I have worked with my neighborhood and local government as a champion and activist, not just for African Americans but for all people who must contend with discrimination. I expect my sons to do the same. I feel that my sons and I are on a mission. It is our duty to help others in our community who are not as fortunate as we are. I never conceived of getting any payment for the time or effort I have put forth in my community. I feel my sons have to do the same thing. If they're going to remain Lees, it's required of them.

I raised my sons to have direction and ambition. I have provided them with good schooling and spent quality time with them. They've always been encouraged and supported in every one of their endeavors, and I don't feel bad reminding them of this. Now, as they have worked along side me and their mother, Kathryn, to build The Observer, one of our nation's strongest African American newspapers, I know they have become capable journalists and capable men.

William Lee, Jr.: Dad's constantly reminding us to use our talents for the betterment of our community and our fellow man. But he practices what he preaches. I believe that he has been a good role model for me.

Larry Lee: Many young African American men in my generation have to fight and struggle to get a job. There are so many pitfalls, with drugs and gangs. I never had to endure these kind of hardships. I didn't get messed-up in the wrong kinds of crowds. But I know how it can happen. I've had hurdles of my own to overcome, but dad taught me that each struggle is an opportunity to learn. I've learned a great deal.

Harold Snook: My father was fifty-five when I was born. Because of that, I didn't have the companionship with him that I would have liked. I vowed that I would not let that happen with my sons. However, with the demands of my law enforcement career, I found there was not sufficient time to remain as active in my boy's lives as I would have liked.

It was during World War II that I began to realize how much influence my father had in shaping me into a man. As I look at all three of my sons, I can see many traits in them that reflect the guidance I attempted to give. I hope, like my own father, that my efforts were somewhat successful.

My boys are all good Christians, who attend church regularly, which I do not. I did not push them in this direction, but I always reminded them that if they questioned their faith, they had only to go out of doors and look at the wonders around them and they would realize that they were a part of a glorious plan.

I taught them how to hunt and how to fish. I taught them that you should take only those things that would be used for food, and to protect those things that were left. I taught them to love God and their Country. In these things I know I was successful.

As I reflect on our lives, I can see that we have some wonderful memories of things we did as a family. I can see how we grew close, then separated somewhat, before returning to the close knit group that we are.

I am glad that none of my sons followed me into law enforcement. Although, I did not attempt to discourage them. When they developed an interest in a field, I tried to provide them with the tools they needed and encouraged them to follow their bent. As a result, they went in separate directions and I am proud of all their accomplishments.

We manage to get together, though too infrequently, to hunt or to fish. I only wish that the boys and their families could go with me to Alaska in the summer and enjoy the wonders of that wonderful state.

The "I" in this discourse has to include my wonderful wife, Barbara, who filled the shoes of father, during the many times I was unavailable, as well as being Mom.

Randy Snook: I love my father. As I was growing up he taught me to work hard, be dedicated to family, and to be a man of integrity. But, I believe the greatest lesson my father taught me was patience, which is quite strange, because he is often very impatient. He taught me this important character trait through our hunting and fishing together. We spent many, many hours waiting for a flight of ducks to go by or a fish to bite while we were on a hunting or fishing excursion. Often our hunting trips would start at five o'clock in the morning, when we would drive to our duck hunting club. We would go out to our blind in the dark, and sit in a submerged concrete tube with our eyes peering between marsh plants, waiting for the birds to make their morning flights. They would normally be flying, but at altitudes usually reserved for airplanes, not birds. We would sit, not talking, just watching and waiting. Then, after sitting there for hours, my dad would say, "Don't worry, I hear a ten o'clock flight is scheduled for today." Ten o'clock would arrive, but still no birds would come. Then it would be lunchtime. We would take a break, talk a little while, have some lunch, and then go back into our secret hiding place, silent, waiting. "I understand a two o'clock flight is scheduled for today." "Yeah, sure dad," I would reply. Two o'clock would come, and still no birds. "Do you want to go home Ran?" "Up to you dad." "Well, let's see what happens when the birds move around at sunset." "Okay dad." Then it would be sunset and a flight would finally come by and my dad would nail one and I would miss. I'm glad he taught me patience, but I wish he would have also taught me how to shoot!

" As I look at all three of my sons, I can see many traits in them that reflect the guidance I attempted to give. I hope, like my own father, that my efforts were somewhat successful."

125

Benny Poon: I remember my father was very strict. I was raised in a very traditional Chinese family. Things are different here in America. In the Chinese culture we respect the teachers and the elders. We are taught to listen, to obey, and to never talk back. That's how I grew up. Over here it is a little different. People are more open. They can express their own feelings. Both ways are good and bad. I think children should have their own way of thinking. But they should not have too many freedoms. Sometimes if they are too free, it can be very difficult to raise them.

I try to teach my children to be obedient, hard working, and responsible. I try to do that by using myself as the example. I do it in this manner, so they can observe and understand the importance of these values. I remember my father always telling me an old saying, "If you don't know how to manage your time, you will not know how to manage your life." I tell my sons the same thing over and over. Now they are starting to grasp the meaning. Especially Eric. He is very good in organizing his schedules, his time, etc. I am very proud of him. I believe that I probably use some of my father's methods subconsciously in raising my boys.

My expectations are high for my two sons. That's why I try to teach them everything I know. They need to be prepared to survive in this society. I want them to become good citizens, to be responsible, respectful, and well educated. I will spend all the money I have for their education. For example, if they want a computer program that will teach them something, I will buy it. If they want to take certain classes that will enrich them, I will sign them up. I have no problem with it as long as I can afford it. I have always told them that I think education is the best investment. But if you want a television set, you will have to buy it yourself.

I try to share our culture with my children, especially the major Chinese holidays. I have explained to them what each holiday means, and we celebrate them as a family. Chinese New Year is equivalent to the American Thanksgiving. Our family gets together for dinner and we say blessings in Cantonese. We give the boys wrapped envelopes with money inside as good luck. Families and friends all give each other gifts to wish them prosperity and good health. This is the culture we want to them to take an interest in. Eric has become more interested in the Chinese culture now that he is older. It has surprised me. When we had him to go to a Chinese class when he was younger, he did not like it. But, now, he seems interested. He'll sometimes ask what a certain verse in Chinese means. Someday I would like to take them both to Hong Kong.

Finally, I hope that they look at me as a loving, responsible father who has tried his best in raising them.

"Fair Play For Fathers," by **P.G. Wodehouse**

The advent of Father's Day in America has inspired the advertisement pages of the magazines to suggestions for brightening the life of this poor underprivileged peon. "Buy him an outboard runabout speedboat 14 foot long with a 62 foot beam," say the magazines. "Buy him a synchromatic wrist watch, water and shock resistant. Buy him a fishing-rod 7 foot long with reinforced ferrules and large-capacity spinning Beachcomber reel," say the magazines, knowing perfectly well that if he gets anything, it will be a tie with pink horseshoes on a blue background.

What he really wants, of course, is a square deal from the hellhounds of Television.

It is difficult to say when the thing started, but little by little the American Father has become established on the Television screen as Nature's last word in saps, boobs and total losses, the man with two left feet who can't make a move in any direction without falling over himself. Picture a rather exceptionally I Q-less village idiot and you will have the idea. Father, as he appears in what is known in Television circles as heartwarming domestic comedy, is a bohunkus who could walk straight into any establishment for the care of the feeble-minded and no questions asked.

There are two sorts of heart-warming domestic comedy on American Television. One deals with the daily doing of the young husband and the young wife who converse for thirty minutes without exchanging a civil word. The other features Father, showing him, to quote a recent writer, as "a miserable chinless half wit with barely enough mechanical skill to tie his own shoes." Almost any domestic crisis will do to make him a mockery and a scorn to twenty million viewers. The one the writer selects is Operation Refrigerator. Mom finds that the refrigerator won't work, and Pop says leave it to him, he'll fix it.

Now Pop, says the writer, may be a mechanic during his working hours-he may even be a refrigerator repair man-but in the home he reverts to the Stone Age. He strews the floor with more parts than there are in six refrigerators and a cyclotron. Then, baffled, he (a) goes berserk, (b) collapses or (c) so assembles the parts that the refrigerator spouts boiling water.

It is at this point that Junior steps forward. Junior is an insufferably bumptious stripling of ten or eleven with a freckled face and a voice like a cement-mixer. He straightens everything out with effortless efficiency, speaking patronizing words to Pop over his shoulder. It is obvious that he regards the author of his being as something that ought not lightly to be allowed at large.

128

I suppose the dim-witted American Father will some day go into the discard like the comic Frenchman with the beard and top-hat and the comic Englishman with the front teeth and whiskers, but it is going to be a grim struggle to get him out of Television. Those Television boys don't often get an idea, but when they do they cling to it. But where they got this idea of the American Child as a mechanical genius it is hard to say.

In the village to which I retire in the summer months the trouble shooters who come round to me when anything goes wrong are grave elderly men in overalls who are obviously experts at their job. I cannot believe that in their homes they have to rely on a freckled child to fix the leaking washer in the scullery tap. I have never come across any mechanically-minded children. Fred Garcia, one of our younger set, has "souped up" his car so that it will do a hundred and thirty m.p.h. and recently covered the fourteen hundred miles between Miami, FL and New York, NY, in thirty hours, which is unquestionably good going; but Fred is eighteen and training to be a jet pilot. Junior in those heart-warming domestic comedies is never more than twelve at the outside. Often he is nearer six, with curls and an all-day sucker.

What the American child *is* good at is dialogue. There he definitely shines. One specimen of the breed in knickerbockers and a Brigade of Guards tie (to which I am almost sure he was not entitled) looked in on me the other day as I worked in the garden and fixed me with an unwinking stare.

"Hi!" he said.

"Hi to you," I responded civilly.

A pause.

"Wotcher doin'?"

"Gardening."

"Oops."

Another pause.

"Have you got a father?" he said.

I said I had not.

"Have you got a mother?"

"No."

"Have you got a sister?"

"No."

"Have you got a brother?"

"No."

"Have you got any candy?"

Crisp. That is the word I was trying to think of. The American child's dialogue is crisp.

Coming back to the American Father, there was the other day just a gleam of light in his darkness. On the Kraft Theatre programme a family was shown having all sorts of family problems, and who should the wise, kindly person who solved them be but Father. It seems incredible, and several people have told me that I must have imagined it or that I switched the thing off before the big scene at the end showing Father trying to fix the electric light. It may be so.

Meanwhile, I think it only right to warn the Television authorities that if they allow things to continue as they are, they are in grave peril. There has been a good deal of angry muttering of late in the Amalgamated Union of American Fathers, and if you ask me, I think the men are about ready to march.

I am watching the situation very closely.

Fair Play For Fathers" by P.G. Wodehouse is reprinted by permission of Punch magazine, Liberty Publishing, London, UK

Ray von Stockhousen: I want my son to know that no matter what happens in his life, or where he's at, or however old he is, that all he has to do is pick up the phone, call me, and I will be there for him. I want no separation between us.

When I was Henk's age my father was out with his hunting buddies, working on cars, or at the bar. My mother divorced him when I was five, she remarried when I was seven and a year later we moved to Hawaii. My dad was in California and we saw less and less of each other until there was no contact for over ten years. My mother remarried, but my relationship with my stepfather wasn't any better than it had been with my real father. I want to make sure that no matter what it takes, that my relationship with my son will be totally different.

When Henk was six months old my wife convinced me to contact my father and invite him up to see his grandson. It was so funny, just the contrast between the two of them. My father's dark complected, with black thick hair and brown eyes. My son has blonde hair and green eyes. It was just beautiful. They looked so different, but it didn't really matter because there was my father and my son, and I was sitting there looking at them, just enjoying the moment.

I want memories for Henk. I have no childhood memories of my father or stepfather doing much of anything with me. Now that Henk is getting older, he's beginning to tell me stories about when we did this or when we did that. Often his stories are just about little trips to the park or Toys 'R Us, but they make me stop and think, "Yeah, I'm doing something right."

Colin Mitchell, *Computer Programmer*
Miles Bennet Mitchell

Colin Mitchell: Becoming a father has brought about an entirely new life for me. It is as though everything that I have done before, is now totally irrelevant. As an expectant father you hope for and would, of course, be happy with any healthy baby. But, I think, it is something special having a son when you're a man. I believe this feeling comes from the knowledge that, in some way, you will continue. Not necessarily by name, but more by nature.

My father and I didn't really have a relationship for most of my childhood. He worked long hours and was often going to school. You know, I don't remember seeing him a whole lot, or doing much with him. It was just me and my mom. Then my parents got divorced when I was ten and that was that. It's only during the past few years that I've really developed a relationship with him. My father and I both got to a point where we decided that we wanted a relationship. We just didn't want to let it go. It's real nice having a relationship with him now. I don't want it to be like that with Miles. I have decided that it is not important to be rich or to have a good job, if I'm not going to have a good relationship with my son. Money and success are not that important. He is the most important thing in my life.

Having a child causes you to undergo changes in your life that are so profound, that they are hard to express in words. Once you have a child, it's like you become a member of this secret society. In fact, there should be a secret handshake or something like that. When I meet other parents now, we don't have to say much. I now understand what they have been talking about all this time.

Craig DiBlasi: One of the wonderful things about having children, is that when they have a great experience, you get to experience it as well. Watching my son experience something for the first time, gives me a greater thrill than when I first had the experience myself. One wonderful memory I have of my son happened during a baseball game. He wasn't a great hitter, and when he occasionally did get a hit, it would be in the infield and result in an out. One day though, he hit one deep in the outfield and got on base. Witnessing his excitement and his sense of accomplishment was so wonderful, I will never forget it.

Adam DiBlasi: My dad shows me he loves me by the stuff that he does. He plays and talks with me. He just talks about me. My favorite thing to do with my dad is to go on a bike ride. We go down hills and through the mud. It's great!

" My favorite thing to do with my dad is to go on a bike ride. We go down hills and through the mud. It's great!"

Warren Dayton, *Illustrator/Designer*
Tad Dayton

Warren Dayton: From the moment Tad came into this realm out of the heart of God, he has been an inquisitive, energetic and joyful person. Our friendship has grown deeper through the nearly fourteen years he has been with me. I am grateful at his open-hearted attitude towards life. His outlook is very positive and he encourages me when I am troubled. It is a joy to be with him, with some of our best times having been spent working together on various projects. I am glad that he would rather be involved in a family activity, than watching television. His enthusiasm for completing something he's making often causes him to forget to put away his tools and keep his room in order (very much like his Papa). Tad loves God and is always ready to pray for whomever is in need. I am thankful beyond words that Jesus put Tad into my life. We have a very unique friendship that God is using to grow each of us into the sons He wants us to be.

Tad Dayton: My father has shown how much he cares for me. He has demonstrated his enduring love for me. When I had once hurt his feelings, he wrote me a letter. This letter was full of beautiful, touching thoughts, where he had expressed his heart's most precious feelings onto paper. I have treasured this letter inside of me and will for ages to come. I love my father with great hope that God will deepen our relationship even more throughout the years.

I remember when I was little he would give me art lessons, since he is an artist, and we would always share our drawings and paintings. We had great fun experimenting with colors and drawings of all types and sizes. We would make up games and activities as we went along. Those happy times have always been special to me. They remind me of how great my father's care for me has always been.

The Mathews Foundation for Prostate Cancer Research

Today the words "prostate cancer" evoke many responses among individuals. From slight concern to outright alarm, from general awareness to all-too-specific insight, from a sense that this is a vague and distant problem to the fear of immediate peril.

Just a few years ago, there was very little public discussion of this terrible disease. Now, largely through the outreach efforts of The Mathews Foundation for Prostate Cancer Research, that situation has changed. But, there is still much to accomplish.

Awareness of this disease and the threat it represents is just beginning to grow. Few people realize that prostate cancer is the only cancer whose incidence has more than tripled during the past seven years, or that it is the number one tumor cancer among men and the number two cancer killer of men.

Statistics show us that every 1.6 minutes an American man will be diagnosed with prostate cancer and every 12.5 minutes and American man will die from this disease. That represents 42,400 deaths and 340,000 new cases diagnosed this year alone. Prostate cancer is not just a problem in the United States, it is at epidemic proportions throughout the world.

Certainly, prostate cancer is not the only health threat which challenges the modern age. It is, though, one of the most serious. In spite of the serious nature of this disease, less than two percent of the National Cancer Institute's medical research budget has been devoted to this deadly cancer. Prostate cancer receives the least funding per patient of all the major cancers. Devoting more of our resources to prostate cancer research needs to be increased for two reasons. The first is that it makes economic sense. Federally expended costs for prostate cancer treatment, lost productivity, and mortality are estimated to soon exceed $6 billion per year. Clearly, finding a solution to this disease is an economically practical goal. But, there is an even more significant imperative. Prostate cancer is a scourge which is robbing our society of some of its most vital human resources. As such, it must be eliminated.

While this disease is often perceived as one which only strikes an older population, the fact is that more than twenty percent of its victims are not yet 65. Of that twenty percent, a startling number of the victims are only in their forties. The brutal twist is that it appears that when the disease does occur at a younger age, it occurs in a more virulent form.

We at The Mathews Foundation feel a sincere obligation to speak out for the prostate cancer patients and their families at every opportunity, so that the world understands the magnitude of this problem and to effectively focus resources to bring about its cure. We have tremendous interest in research on this disease and the way that traditional research is funded. Working together is the best, most efficient and productive way to institute the changes that are necessary to eliminate this disease...for our fathers and our sons.

Sincerely,

Mary Lou Wright

Mary Lou Wright
President and Chief Executive Officer

If you would like additional information about prostate cancer, or if you would like to further assist the Mathews Foundation in their efforts, please call 1-800-234-6284.

Participation Opportunity

The next book that photographer Randy Snook will be working on is tentatively titled, "My Father, My Hero." This book will be similar in format to "Fathers & Sons," but will focus on both sons and daughters and why they believe that their father is a "hero." Our desire is to illustrate a variety of fathers who are heroes for different reasons. These reasons would include risking ones life for others, overcoming great obstacles to carry out the responsibilities of fatherhood, showing integrity when being pressured not to, and many others. If you believe that your father is a "hero," we would like to include you, your father, and your story in this upcoming tribute. Please fax your story for consideration to Visual Press, at 916-739-6230. I hope that you will join us in this exciting project!

Contact information:

Randy Snook Photography

(916) 455-1360

email visual@tomatoweb.com

Diane Sutherland Art Direction

(916) 933-1513

email dsad@aol.com

Order Form

Yes! I like Fathers & Sons so much that I want to order extra copies.

To order:

Call toll free 1-888-641-4DAD

Fax this form to: 916-739-6230

Mail to: Visual Press
3385 Lanatt St., Suite B
Sacramento, CA 95819

Item	Quantity	Price	Total
Fathers & Sons (softcover) *$23.95*		$23.95	
Fathers & Sons (hardcover) *$49.95*		$49.95	
Subtotal			
CA residents add 7.75% sales tax			
Shipping ($4 for the first book & $2 for each additional)			
Total			

Please ship my order to:

Name_____

Address_____

City_____State_____Zip_____

Daytime Phone: (_____)_____

Payment: ☐ Check (made payable to Visual Press)
☐ Credit card: ☐ Visa ☐ MasterCard

Card number: _____

Signature: _____

Name on card:_____ Exp. date:_____